GW00456850

Finding Good

The products, the makers, the heritage, the traditions, the pubs, the events, the social, the drinkers and the fun

A year in the life of a cider lover in the West Country

By Alan Stone

Plus 'Finding Good Cider in the age of the Scientific Revolution'

By Dr Richard Stone

Published in 2016 by

Somersethistory.co.uk

sheptonhistory@btinternet.co.uk

10 Society Road, Shepton Mallet BA4 5GF

Printed by Remous, Wyvern Buildings, Glovers Close, Milborne Port, Sherborne, Dorset DT9 5EP

ISBN 978-0-9572611-6-7

Cover design nige reece – managing director of Cognique, www.cognique.co.uk
Whose first attempt at cider making was most impressive

Introduction to 'Finding Good Cider'

This book is somewhat different to my previous cider books. It has tried to go beyond being a gazetteer of local cider makers and notes on history. In this book I have attempted to come up with a concept of 'good cider' and explore this idea.

'Good cider' is not just about cider as a product – though what it is and what makes some ciders better than others forms a huge part of it! It is not just about artisan producers and it is certainly not about criticising large scale producers – cider is a broad church – the important thing is that people explore, enjoy and understand what they are drinking.

'Good cider' is also not just about the producers. As I say I have not set out to produce a gazetteer. This is largely a record of my cider experiences in 2015 and the first quarter of 2016. Mainly presented in a rough chronological order throughout the year is does also go off at tangents and it is not presented as a continuous timeline as I explore different topics or update previously mentioned items.

Not being a Gazetteer means that not all cider producers are mentioned. It is not intended to be a 100% guide book. It is a record of what I have come across during the year that fits into my personal view of 'good cider'. Although I have ranged across the West County there are some parts I just didn't get to – and confess this in the book. Not being mentioned definitely should not be taken as criticism. However, as the book shows, I have mentioned quite a lot of producers!

The concept of 'good cider' explored in this book goes much further than product and producers. It covers the shows and festivals where good cider is part of the lifeblood and many people are enjoying it. It also covers pubs which not only serve good cider but have a wonderful atmosphere.

'Good cider' encompasses the heritage of cider and its living tradition and also the orchards that provide the raw materials.

'Good cider' is part of the beating heart of the West County and for some of us an essential refuge as away from our busy lives in a modern world.

Contents

Disclaimer

Every effort has been made to make sure the information in this book is accurate. However in a market place an diverse and changing as the artisan cider making it is inevitable that some errors will have crept in.

The overstated opinions expressed throughout are those of the author – however they should always be taken with a pinch of salt. The whole ethos of the book is to encourage people to go out and explore for themselves and form their own opinions with a bit more knowledge than before.

Finding good cider is part of the fun side of life – please do not take it too seriously!

Thanks

I would like to thank all those producers and cidermakers who generously gave me so much time and help with this book. Although I do not like to single out one I feel I do have to make a special mention of passionate cider lover Bob Cork whose experience with a large scale cider makers gave me an extra perspective on the industry.

I would also like to thank my cidermaking historian son Richie – or Dr R.G.Stone as he likes to be known nowadays. Not only did he share a number of my adventures – he also contributed an excellent chapter on early cider production. I am already trying to think of my response to the many people who are bound to tell me it is the most important bit of the book.

I must also thank my wife Christine for not only proof reading but also encouraging me to remove my worst excesses from the text.

Talk at the Somerset Food and Drink Festival 18 October 2015 at the Bath and West Showground

An introduction to cider

Good afternoon

Here in my hand, the observant amongst you will have spotted, what is commonly known as an apple. In this case it is a Kidds Orange with its distinctive conical shape. It is a distinctive eating apple with good storing properties – one of my favourites which I have picked for many years at the pick your own orchards of Edward Clifton Brown just down the road at West Bradley.

Cider according to the dictionary is the fermented juice of apples. Such a definition includes all apples – unfortunately the juice from this apple is not very good for making a 'good cider' but more of that in a minute.

Please ignore the particular variety of this apple and pretend we are going to make cider from it anyway. The first task is to get the juice out of it. You will notice that however hard I squeeze it in my hand I don't make much of an impressions on it. Obviously there has to be some sort of special technique to get the juice out. This involves chopping it up very small and applying pressure. A kitchen mixer of some sort should do the trick. At home, having burnt out a couple of blenders, juicers, or whatever you want to call them, I can assure you this is not a bright idea on any scale. Some people wait until the apples are very ripe and soft and then pound them in a bucket with a heavy fence post or lumps of wood, this is extremely hard work.

Most cider makers who want to make more than a few litres will be using a 'mill' or 'scratter' of some sort. Ours looks like a garden shredder and has a big yellow funnel. Unlike a garden shredder the blades do not rotate horizontally to chop but it has a cunningly shaped vertical blade which rotates *(twiddles first finger round and round to demonstrate!)*

Out of the bottom of the mill comes the apples chopped up into a porridge like constituency – the pomace. It has started to look distinctly moist but is still far from being 'juice'. Now we need the press to squeeze the juice out. I recently saw someone put some pomace in a cheesecloth and squeeze with bare hands. Yes, he got a bit out but not a lot! You need a press. For the hobby maker there are many on the market – mainly those attractive basket presses where there is a 'basket' of upright staves which you fill up with the pomace, put a lid on and screw down. The juice collects in a tray at the bottom and then drains into a container to catch it – lovely, sweet apple juice.

These presses are fine for a limited quantity. You can get bigger ones though the usual route is to progress to the traditional rack and cloth presses where you build a 'cheese' of layers of pomace wrapped in muslin with straw or racks separating the layers. In these presses you apply serious pressure from the top – I used to use a 24 tonne bottle jack. This type of press provides us with the usual images of traditional farmhouse cider making.

There are other variants – many have been mechanised with hydraulics. I currently use a hydro press where water from a hose fills a bladder down the centre of a basket type press, it is great fun to see the juice rush out as if by magic when you turn the tap on. Or you can go to much larger scale type belt presses where the price tag starts at about £20,000 for a small one. Then there are the massive high powered Bucher presses you will find in the biggest cider mills.

At the end of this process the quantity of juice that has been got out of our apple is equivalent to roughly 70% of the whole apple. 10 kilograms of apple should provide about 7 litres of juice. Though in practice the amateur with less than perfect equipment may have to be satisfied with about 5 litres.

You now have some very sweet tasting apple juice. You could drink this as it is – very nice. Or you could put it in plastic lemonade bottles and put in the freezer. Or you could pasteurise and bottle it. What you cannot do is just put it in a bottle and leave it to drink more than a day or two later. A natural fermentation will start and carbon dioxide (CO_2) will build up which will burst virtually any type of container you care to mention – especially glass bottles – and depending how close you were to the explosion you may or may not have eyes left to see it.

For cider the juice should be put into a container that allows CO_2 to escape but stops spoilage bacteria coming in. The wine making demijohn with an airlock is the usual starting solution and it is then only a matter of scale to achieve the same result.

A fermentation will usually start within a few days. This basically converts the sweetness – sugars – in the apple juice to alcohol – the cider. Some producers swear by using wild yeasts that are present in the environment – especially where cider has been made before. Most of us would rather add a special yeast to ensure the fermentation is the sort of fermentation we want driven by the right sort of yeasts.

The fermentation will take between three weeks and six months depending in the main on the temperature. Once the fermentation has stopped the cider will be dry and stable. You need to 'rack' it off the lees – carefully removing the cider from the layer of dead yeast and other sediment from the original pressing of the fruit. Leave to mature and develop its flavour for a couple more months and with a lot of luck (or skill as many claim) you will have a drinkable cider which you can sweeten to taste – more on this later.

This is basically how you make cider – though there are a lot of instruction manuals that can take you into it in a great deal more cider – my son and I have found Craft Cidermaking by Andrew Lea is by far and away the best – a new edition has come out in 2015.

Artisan Cider makers.

My main interest is in the so called 'Artisan Cider' makers who make 'good cider'. Quite what an Artisan Cider maker is no two people would seem to ever agree. I will for now stick at suggesting it is a 'not in a factory' cider maker. Most artisan cider makers fundamentally follow the sort of simple production technique above and produce a cider that is as near as dam it made from 100% apple juice. The artisan cider maker will be someone who takes a pride in his craft and probably makes between 4,000 and 100,000 litres of cider a year. My son and I are just off the bottom of this scale – we both work very full time so for us it is more of a hobby. We are registered with HMRC as wholesalers. You can see our stand in the festival here and also that of Neil Worley of Worley's cider who is another artisan cider maker but one who is trying to make a living out if it by making about 50,000 litres – and he makes some excellent ciders. A common trait for artisan producers is a passion for their product.

To a avoid confusion it is important to point out that not all cider made by smaller makers is necessarily 'good cider' and cider made by factory cider makers can also be 'good cider.'

The process followed by artisan makers is very much the traditional cider making process which would have been a natural part of farming life in the West Country for the past 500 or 600 years. Unfortunately in the latter 19th and for most of the 20th century there was not a lot of money in cider and many of the farmhouse ciders suffered from a distinct lack of interest from the farmers and the sour vinegar like 'scrumpy' ciders abounded along with the legends of dead rats and other unsavoury practices. Some farmworkers and some others seem to have developed a taste for this product. It can still be found even today on farms quite close to here. However, there were always other cider makers who were interested in the quality of the product they produced and the fine tradition of West Country Ciders has re-emerged strongly over the past 20 years.

Another descriptor is 'farmhouse cider.' Unfortunately not all farmhouse cider makers are artisan – there is a need for interest in the product to be artisan. And although many artisan cider makers are based on farms by no means all are. To me the most important thing is access to the right apples.

Cider apples

The essential ingredient for making an artisan cider is cider apples. There are over 350 types of cider apple that have been identified and are propagated in England. The major skill of the artisan cider maker is in the selection of the right varieties and blends of cider apples. It is the properties of these apples that is behind the secret of 'good cider' - a natural product.

There is a romance behind the names of many of the genuine cider apples. Kingston Back is probably the most famous, mainly as it is the best cider apple for making a single variety cider,that is not blended with other varieties. Other well-known apples growing locally include Yarlington Mill and Harry Masters Jersey from a few miles down the road at Yarlington – just the other side of Castle Cary. Harry Masters was the miller at Yarlington Mill and the seedling of Yarlington Mill was reputedly found growing out of the wall of the mill.

Another very popular cider apple is Dabinett. This possibly accounts for nearly a third of all cider apples grown commercially in England and is a very essential constituent of many ciders both artisan and commercial. Despite its French sounding name 'Dabinett' is a Somerset variety. At a cider event in Hinton St George Village Hall in South Somerset I saw a memorial board to the villagers who died in the Great War. A good number of them were named Dabinett. I was once with cider making legend Julian Temperley at his Burrow Hill orchard. The view was of almost unbroken orchards and he pointed out into the distance to Middle Lambrook where the original Dabinet apple tree was found growing out of a wall.

It may be important to point out that although we all know apples have pips from which apple trees grow that the trees grown from pips do not grow true to variety. If you find a seedling that has produced an interesting apple you then need to propagate it on through cuttings and grafting. The vast majority of seedlings do not produce apples that are suitable for much at all.

Other varieties include the more obscure names such as – such as Sack-me-girdle, Cap of Liberty, Cider Ladies Finger, Fair Maid of Taunton and many many more. Identifying the variety of apples on trees you come across in old orchards is extremely challenging, even for the experts, and the experience of pomologist Liz Copas who lives near Crewkerne is sought after by all. Like most cider makers I have well-thumbed copies of her books where the photographs are an initial but fallible starting point. You may think the photograph of an apple variety looks just right, but then read the text and find that other aspects do not match up – maybe the apple is only grown in the West of Cornwall – or it has only recently been identified in an overgrown orchard in Dorset.

From the wide choice of cider varieties most have been identified as belonging to one of four particular categories of cider apple. These are based on the ratio of tannin to acid in the fruit. The four are
1. Sharps – which have high acidity but low tannin
2. Bittersharps – which have high acidity and high tannins
3. Bittersweets – which have low acidity but high tannins
4. Sweets – which have low acidity and low tannins.

Nearly all the good ciders are made of blends of one or more of these types of apple. Cookers such as Bramley may be considered an extreme version of a sharp – dessert apples may be more like sweets – though many desserts are quite acidic.

To most West Country cider makers the most defining element is the level of tannin. It is this that gives the complexity of taste and the 'mouthfeel' of a good cider. Here though is a further level of confusion – it is not just the overall level of tannin. Apples like Tremlets Bitter have a hard tannin which can almost be uncomfortable for the novice to drink whereas other bittersweet apples like Dabinett have a much more pleasant soft tannin and a fresh feel in the mouth.

One important thing to note is that 'sweet' apples certainly do not make sweet cider. This is very commonly misunderstood even by some experienced amateur makers and commentators. All cider apples naturally ferment out dry and then have sweetness added back in or a small number of cases use complex procedures to help retain an element of residual sweetness. Ciders made with 'sweet' apples may be softer in taste – and the addition of sweetness seems to work well but fundamentally please do not fall into the trap of thinking that apples like Morgan Sweet, Sweet Alford or Sweet Coppin will necessarily result in a sweet cider.

Okay that is one layer of complication. The next is that many of the cider apple varieties have their own distinctive taste. Somerset Redstreak is meant to have a slight peppery taste. Kingston Black is easily recognised. Morgan Sweet has a pleasant distinctive though thin taste. Julian Temperly of Burrow Hill Cider and many others would very strongly argue that the best ciders are made of blends of at least eight different cider apples. The variation in taste of particular varieties means that the making of single variety ciders can be very rewarding. However, apart from Kingston Black most single variety ciders benefit from adjusting either the tannin or the acidity as well as the sweetness.

Just to complicate things even more! The taste of a particular variety can vary from orchard to orchard. The local 'terroir' can make a significant difference. Old timers are said to have been able to identify which orchard particular ciders were made from.

If you have managed to grasp this as a concept now please try to get you head around the fact that the same variety in the same orchard can vary from year to year depending on the weather during the growing season!

Making good cider is a real art!

'Now who would like a pint of cider?' (*Holds out pint glass to audience and pours less than an inch in the bottom*)

'What – don't you think that is a pint?'

Remembering that cider is supposed to be fermented apple juice that may be all the apple juice you get in some of the most popular brands of cider. One of the lager linked brands of cider the other year was proudly claiming on their website that it contained 17.5% of real juice. Many artisan producers would expect good cider to be approaching 100% apple juice from cider apples.

It is questionable that cider with 17.5% juice should legally be called cider. Only a few years ago a regulation was introduced suggesting that cider had to contain at least 33% apple juice. Unfortunately this was 33% at a lower level of sugar than most cider apples naturally contain and as the measuring of juice is done by measuring the sugar level the large scale factory cider makers soon realised that they could get away with 19% apple juice within this regulation. Some people were quite suspicious that the world's leading cider brand made in Hereford seemed to have the word 'cider' removed from all its labelling for a couple of years.

'Okay then – that is not the sort of cider you want.' *(Adds another inch of juice into the pints glass).* 'There that's better isn't it?'

What – still feeling short changed? Having talked to many people 40% apple juice is about the level that many commercially produced ciders from our national manufacturers would contain. There is nothing wrong with this. They make very pleasant drinks.

What is the rest I hear you ask? Well basically water. The strength is kept up by fermenting the juice with glucose syrup and other sugars – hence references to industrial cider as 'glucose wine.' Corn starch, invert sugars, malic acid, industrial alcohols, sweeteners and other cheap additives are alleged to be used. A nameless cider producer once gave me a boasting talk of how few pence he could produce a pint of cider for – way below the cost of the juice of pressed cider apples.

'Does this matter?', after all cider is a very popular well received summer drink?

In reality a lot of the ultra-low juice ciders taste very thin. They are either a bit 'tinny' or more usually sickly sweet and distinctly taste more of sweetener than cider. This is not new practice. Someone suggested that if 'traditional' could be taken as meaning a generation of 30 years then it has certainly been going on for far longer than that – definitely back to the 19th century. Some of the better ones are very pleasant drinks – I drink quite a lot of them when 100% juice ciders are not available. Though actually I am more likely to drink a real ale!

What matters is that the marketing of these ciders can be misleading. Nearly every large commercial producer bases their brand around the idea that cider is a natural product, with repeated images of apples growing on the trees in orchards and on the traditional rural heritage of cider with oak barrels and farm workers. A very good examples of this was the long running adverts based on the idea that farm workers at haymaking time would search out the farmers who made the best cider with which to quench their thirst. There will have been some truth behind the idea that some farmers made better cider than others – but as an interpretation of social history considering options open to the agricultural labourer in the second half of the 19th century and first half of the 20th century this is way off the harsh realities of rural life.

Then there advertising around cider stored in oak. Of course in former days just about all cider was fermented and stored in oak barrels. It was all there was. And yes fresh oak barrels certainly can impart some flavours to cider. This is not a given rule. Oak barrels can allow air into contact with cider speeding up its 'going off'. They can introduce also off flavours. Most current producers do not use oak vats – preferring stainless steel if they can afford it – or plastic if they can't. However, the marketing men for certain big producers insist on perpetuating the fallacy that it is essential it is stored in wood. On a guided tours of a large commercial producer they reveal that some of their ciders do in fact pass through huge oak vats which are used as holding tanks – sometimes for as little as a few days. What difference can this possible make to the cider? These Vats are often 50 or 100 years old. There is no possibility of them affecting the taste of the cider with the millions of gallons that have passed through them. Yet if you see a photograph or TV advertisements they are likely to loom large as being the essence of their cider!

There is some evidence that commercial manufacturers are hiding the truth from consumers. When you come across a bottle of cider for export you discover they have an ingredients list which often contains quite a lot of small print with different preservatives, taste enhancers and varied sweeteners. Why does this not get included on labels for the British market? If you look at many manufactured food stuffs they will have against the ingredients the percentage of each. You can look for vain on cider labels as to what percentage of apples or even apple juice has been included in the product. You can also look in vain for the source of the ingredients – the country of origin. We know that a lot of cider by some commercial manufacturers – and not necessarily the largest – comes from apple juice that has been concentrated with water then added back in. But where does this concentrate come from? Traditionally a lot came from France, Spain and our other European neighbours. Today a lot comes from Turkey and other eastern European countries – and now increasingly from the huge Chinese orchards. Most of these are definitely not from traditional cider orchards with their rich range of varieties containing the essential blend of acids and tannins. Nor can this be reintroduced through additions to the juice, water and sweetener blend. I should here pint out that many of our larger commercial producers also concentrate their own juice from cider apples they have grown or have had grown for them. Although not a fan of any concentrate you have to be realistic. It is only through concentrating their own juice that these producers can have the space to maintain all year around production.

Does this matter? – after all I freely admit that the best of the products made under these circumstances of often very pleasant, fizzy alcoholic drinks, and most of them well received by a public which would call itself discerning. Should the fact that they don't know what they are drinking but like it be used as a justification?

Why does it matter? We live in an age where there is increasing attention, and much foodie marketing, around transparency in food. What it is, where it comes from, how it is produced – its provenance? Nowadays if you go to a supermarket you can often find information as to which poultry farm the eggs had come from or which herd of cows your milk had come from and how it is produced. Of course it is by no means 100% but supermarkets are realising that there is commercial advantage in being honest about the provenance of their products. People are looking for 'genuine' products. Yet commercial cider makers seem determined to pull the wool over people's eyes. Trumpeting a rich rural natural product, suggesting tradition and heritage of which there is little left. In fact they are not even willing to say what continent it comes from.

Why is this very important? The fact is that there are a lot of producers who do make really good cider with approaching 100% of the juice coming from specialist cider apples of real character and flavour grown in local orchards that are such an important part of our landscape. These producers may use modern equipment but they press their cider in the autumn and leave it to ferment naturally throughout the winter so it is ready for the next spring and summer.

They do not have the option of just cooking up another batch from concentrate when they need it throughout the year.

Of course the intensive marketing of cider has led to marginally increased popularity for all cider products and some smaller producers have been able to benefit – though all too often this has been through mimicking some aspects of products which a purist may not consider desirable. However the sad truth is that the large commercial producers, largely by hiding the truth about their products have managed to hold on to the brand integrity of cider whilst gaining a competitive advantage in terms of margin that stifles the growth of smaller producers who actually are making the products that the marketing men promote. I don't know the exact sums thought roughly would seem to be that the production costs of large scale commercial producers are on average less than 30% of that of the artisan producer with near 100% juice. I can remember talking to a factory producer of the less reputable sort – making three litre bottles of white cider for the corner shops - when I wrote my first cider book. He quickly ran through the sums and if I remember correctly his costs were about a 15th of the costs of an artisan craft maker.

Yes – this does matter! There are craft producers making good cider with the traditional ingredients in the traditional way. A lot of this is very good cider indeed. I urge all of you to go and try it. In this small food festival just behind me you have our own Stone's Bittersweet Cider, from Shepton Mallet three miles up the road. In fact the perry is made of pears grown on this show site just 200 yards away. That is a provenance that takes some beating. Next to our stand is Worley's cider from Dean – four miles away up the road towards Frome. I was present a couple of weeks ago when they won the cider award at the huge Taste of the West food and drink awards ceremony. If you want to go our hunting for cider please find the Hecks, Wilkins, Rich's, Burrowhill, Bere Cider, Honeypot Cider and many more – all within 20 miles. There are a number of local pubs which now have a range of bag in the box ciders from local producers. There is a really rich heritage of great, good cider on your door step – please go out and find it!

(Speaker sits down to thunderous applause – oh if only!)

The start of the year

What better place to start this journal than Boxing Day 2014. Shaking off the sloth and excess of Christmas day with some bracing fresh air. We, wife, cider making elder son Richie and I, went across to Beckery near Glastonbury where we picked up our second son James and his then girlfriend's father Jean Luc – who as you may guess from his name is French, and does not speak more than the odd word of English. In France Jean Luc is a potato contractor, very much a man of the soil and the countryside so we decided to go for a drive over the Somerset Moors and find somewhere to have a drink.

Our first port of call was to the Greylake nature reserve near Othery. On a grey day with a fair bit of rain it was highly atmospheric at this time of year and the fresh weather was ideal for getting the cobwebs out of the system. As we went for the walk to the bird hide it became obvious that the country man Jean Luc was impressed with the amount and selection of wildfowl on display and mimicked shooting them with a shot gun. With his limited English and our limited French explaining that as this was a nature reserve was so shooting was not really an option was rather challenging. And rather pointless as we soon heard the shots of people wildfowling on an adjoining moor.

This is 'real' Somerset as featured in local literature, the Somerset of 'Bond of Green Withy' or the books of Walter Raymond. Whether you refer to the flat boggy landscape fringed with low hills as Moors or Levels does not really matter it is a magical part of the country and is steeped in cider tradition. On almost every hill you will find an old orchard and in some of the local pubs you will find as strong a sense of cider tradition as anywhere else in the country.

As the weather was a mite on the catchy side we decided to find a drink. We paid a visit to Bere Cider, a small artisan cider producer between Othery and Aller. I have previously written about Bere cider in my book 'In Search of Cider'. The farmer Jim Lockyer is a real traditional Somerset character though the quality of their farmhouse cider is probably more the responsibility of son in law Chris Smolden who masquerades as an Insurance and financial planning consultant for a day job. Chris has raised the standard and they now make a very fine farmhouse cider. We were delighted that Jim was there and willing with enthusiasm to give us some tastings of cider even though it was before lunch on the morning of Boxing Day.

Jean Luc was obviously slightly underwhelmed by the still farmhouse cider so he tried the bottled 'Gold Rush' cider which had been mildly carbonated – much more to his taste. We bought a tray of this as it certainly is a pleasant drink. It is important to remember that genial and accommodating as they are Cider farms are there to sell cider not just to hand out tastings. You come across people who from their attitude seem to give the impression that they are doing the farmer a favour by tasting his cider and who have no intention of buying any at all. If we go to a cider maker and taste we expect to find one that suits our tastes and buy some. I always insist on paying something – after all when tasting cider people should recognise that there is a cost to the producer and expect to either buy or give something in return.

Bere Cider is really well set out. They have an excellent hydraulic press in a barn on one side of the yard surrounded by 1000 litre IBCs (tanks) full of recently pressed cider. On the other side of the yard is a former milking parlour with their previous traditional screw press. Beyond this they have over the past few years set up a bar area for serving tastings and a bit of a shop where off sales and souvenirs can be bought. They do not currently have an on licence, where you can buy drinks in glasses and drink them, but Jim is generous with his tastings. Although they may not have built up the reputation of some other famous farm house cider venues this has become one of my favourites – despite the fact that over the past couple of years it has often been inaccessible following the famous floods the winter of 2013/2014 and the subsequent drawn out clearing and then rebuilding of the Othery to Langport road.

Following this we thought we would take Jean Luc to one of the best Somerset pubs. The Halfway House at Pitney. The pub was packed with a Boxing Day lunchtime trade but we were lucky enough to find seats around a shared trestle table. This pub has for the past decade or so specialised in Real Ales and Ciders drawn from the barrels out behind the bar. There is always something good to drink and on this visit we focused on some of the Porters, dark beers. They do usually do some really good pub food today but we tried to sustain ourselves with some packs of fancy crisps.

The Halfway House was one of the first of the modern generation of country pubs in the county, a model that has now been repeated in a good scattering of pubs. Not overly foodie but providing good wholesome pub meals, a great atmosphere and as mentioned as free houses they have an excellent range of beers and are the most likely place to find a selection of good ciders. In terms of finding good ciders I am sure I will be mentioning a good number of these pubs in the coming pages and hopefully list those I have found in the index.

Jean Luc appeared slightly overwhelmed by it and the atmosphere. By the time we got him back he was in a mellow mood. When back with French speakers it was later reported he would not stop talking and was most impressed that we had gone into a pub that was like someone's house. Discussing with James I discovered that even in rural France there is no comparison between their bars and these character pubs with their low ceilings, small rooms, rustic furniture and friendly atmosphere. We are pleased when we discover a good one – but take it for granted that there are others out there when they are really are an English rural institution with no direct comparison elsewhere. To me they really are an essential part of our heritage, if a modern evolution of it, and they fully fit with the culture of 'good cider'.

What a pub should be

Many visits to pubs are pleasant enough but rather run of the mill. Meeting people you know for a drink and a chat, hopefully some decent beer, perhaps a meal if that is what you have gone for, though this can be expensive. Nothing wrong with these but these are the 'run of the mill' things.

However, just occasionally a trip to the pub transcends all expectations and you really believe that if the experience could be repeated more often there would be no problems with our pubs having to close through being underused.

On a Saturday afternoon in mid-January my son Richie and I made the trip out to The Sheppey at Godney to deliver a 20 litre bag in box of our Stone's Bittersweet cider. If you have not been to this pub it is worth if for location alone. You have to go 3 or 4 miles (depending on direction) down very narrow lanes right out into the middle of the Somerset Moors. Flat lands with muddy cattle and pollarded willows. For the last mile or so the lane runs beside the 'River Sheppey' which was far fuller than usual and we speculated on how much more rain it could take before we have some of the flooding as had beset this part of the country the previous winter. From the outside this pub is rather unprepossessing – you have to know it is there and check the door handle to see if it is open. Once inside people are amazed. It is a large open dining pub come restaurant and outside it has a riverside terrace.

However, the bar is small and cluttered with a truly exciting array of drinks – including behind you a rack with about 10 different real ciders – the destination for our box of Stone's Bittersweet. Opposite the bar is a seating area and along from there a snug where drinkers feel they are in a pub not the restaurant – though actually the off-the-wall décor, posters and artwork, background jazz music or a live performance give this pub an atmosphere of its own throughout.

The bar is a treasure trove. Usually half the beers seem to have homemade or temporary pump clips. There is a right mixture of keg taps and hand pumps – or boxes for the cider. The selection includes a really rich mix of real ales, real ciders, lagers, keg ciders and an exciting selection of the new style craft beers. Be careful not to ask the price of the latter, just buy and drink to savour the experience – but for fiscal reasons it may be best to start with a half!

Despite our enthusiasm for cider it is one of these craft beers that we start on, a Coconut Porter from the Bath Ales craft sub-brand, Beerd brewery in Bristol. Porters have thankfully made a great comeback in the past couple of years. Smooth tasting there is a lot of innovation around flavour with some of these porters and this is definitely no exception. A wonderful beer though it is a bit of a shame that because it is in a Beerd Keg it has to go through a chiller – Porter should be best served at room temperature.

The first conversation of the afternoon was a discussion with the bar staff about the origins of the name porter. They had previously been discussing it and the thought was that it was something to do with sailors needing a full bodied beer when they get their ships back into port. I was of the opinion that it was something to do with the porters at the big London markets like Smithfield and Billingsgate. I haven't checked – it was a good discussion and for the sake of a good discussion you don't need be too sure of your facts. I also introduced the subject of the 'new' Guinness original recipe porters. Their 6.5% West Indian Porter is something special.

We had sat down opposite the bar – in the rather terrifying picnic chairs – not designed for my bulk! There was a chap on his own next to us who we said hello to and explained about our Stone's Bittersweet Cider which he had seen us put in the rack. He then got into a conversation with three men at the bar who were talking about doing up old bikes and needing a workshop. The guy next to us said it was a small world and that he had a collection of old bikes and would be willing to let them use his workshop if they did some maintenance work on his collection which he never got around to. It may be hard to believe in such co-incidences but that happens all the time if you are in a pub which is what a pub should be!

With the conversation now including everyone in the bar I suggested that the chap might be interested in exhibiting some of his vintage bikes in the Heritage Tent which I run at the Mid Somerset Show in August. He didn't seem adverse to the idea and introduced himself as 'Gammy' though this was spelt 'Dave Sparkes' on the card he wrote out for me to get in touch with him. The bar thinned out a bit but as Gammy bought a pint of our cider to try – he had been on the Wilkin's – we went onto cider to keep him company. To be fair we were pleased with our cider which we had blended that morning. Based on 2013

Dabinett SV which tasted clean but slightly lacking in character we mixed it with about 25% of 2014(New season) Morgan's Sweet which certainly added some complexity and character to the flavour.

The conversation carried on and two more couples coming in who made the mistake of looking at the cider rack whilst being served and took up our recommendation of trying the Stone's Bittersweet. We discovered that Gammy and I had a common acquaintance in one of my work colleagues from the village of Burtle where Gammy lives. He wanted to know if Neil was ever going to return the football shirt he had taken home to wash 15 years before!

Conversation continued to flow and there was another half before we eventually got away, there is no way you should drink too much with the winding lane beside the river in the dark.

Feeling very relaxed, having met new people and had some amazing conversations we drove home and explained why we had been so long. But it was worth it. Drinking good beer and cider, meeting interesting new characters and taking part in some random but interesting conversations – this is what a pub should be. And is an essential part of the 'finding good cider' mix.

As we are talking about good cider pubs, a number make a backdrop to the year ahead, I better fill you in on a couple of my favourite locals. Two in particular also take our cider regularly. The George in Croscombe is only a couple of miles from where I live – just a bit too far for a comfortable walk – especially as coming back is up hill. Canadian landlord Peter Graham and his wife Veryan have been there for more than a dozen years and have transformed what was a rather ordinary pub into one of the best around and which frequently win's CAMRA awards. It is a great pub for beer, cider and food. They have endured our development as cider makers with exploding bag in boxes, leaking bag in boxes and even taps coming out of bag in boxes and flooding the bar area. It is a pub where we frequently go to eat for family celebrations and I also go for business lunches and Shepton Mallet Chamber of Commerce committee meetings. It the nearest thing to a local I have and in the course of a year I spend far more here that I receive from cider sales!

It is another pub with a great atmosphere and a range of events and festivals during the year. The locals tend to gather around the bar and the conversations are often suitably bizarre. They have two beers made for them – the 'George' and 'George and Dragon' and they have a wide variety of guest beers. Usually this includes a porter or dark beer. They also stock a wide range of ciders. For keg ciders you have two from Thatchers – a few of the locals insist on their 'Cheddar Valley' possibly under the illusion that this is a genuine farmhouse product. There is 'Rattler' cider, a rare surprise this far from Healy's Cornish Cider farm where it is produced. And then there is Pilton Cider from excellent local maker Martin Berkeley. He focuses on champagne bottles of keeved cider but also experiments with kegs and it makes an interesting change from the larger producers.

There is also an interesting bag in box range. At the moment we seem to be providing Stone's Dry as Peter wants a cider that has no additives of any sort in it. I am not sure if he realises what is in all of the other ciders he stocks but we are happy to supply what he wants. Neil Worley is another cider maker providing an excellent bag in box. Then there is usually a box or two of the Orchard Pig Ciders which despite their original 'rural' image is currently being produced in the Shepton Cider Mill. Through the year you will find other boxes from different producers in there. Sometimes these have come through wholesalers who have 'sold' a story to Peter and these boxes may hang around on his shelves for a rather long time!

The third pub which regularly has Stone's ciders is the Travellers Rest on the A37 at Pennard about five miles towards Yeovil from Shepton Mallet. Ian Newman is the landlord here and it is an excellent village local with the slight problem of not having a village! It has Doom Bar as an excellent ale and does food all day every day which largely provides locals and traveller passing on the main road. Pubs like this are would strike you as likely victims of the reduced trade for pubs and the problems with drink drive. This one survives through the energy and enthusiasm of the landlord and his wife apart from each having a separate day off a week are usually ever present. Twice a year one of the regulars takes a week off his work to allow them to go on holiday.

They have succeeded in building up a regular clientele. Their early evening on the way home trade is good. In the evening there are skittles, darts and pool teams. There is sport on a big TV screen frequently showing horse racing and with the nearby stables of Paul Nicholls horses are a frequent backdrop to conversation.

His regular cider was for many years Fosseway Cider from Phil Briggs who lives a couple of hundred yards up the road. This was always a good fruity cider but Phil rather lost interest through having to work full time as well and then had a rather indifferent batch. It disappeared for a while. However in late 2015 it reappeared with Phil being helped by Ian Stalworthy – the local who provides the holiday cover for the landlord. His job as a salesman enables him to distribute help Paul the cider and after a gap of a year or so they have started to make again, getting it pressed on the same mill as myself and Martin Berkeley.

The Travellers Rest also has Paul Chant's ciders bag in box. A very traditional style farmhouse ciders for the brave. This is the sort of cider that tourists buy to take away with them back home where they can give it to their friends to show how brave they are trying genuine West Country Cider. Not for me. The Travellers Rest occasionally has some other guest ciders. I had some excellent cider from John Lawrence at Corton Denham there last summer.

A recent addition to the pubs that have had Stone's Cider is the Full Moon tucked away down a back street in Wells behind Morrisons. Shaun the landlord has a few ciders based around Wilkin's Dry from Roger Wilkins at Mudgely – a local cider maker of legendary status. As they turn it over quite quickly it stays fresh. In fact they stopped doing the Wilkin's Sweet as it was not selling so fast and they were ending up with half barrels of sour cider. The solution is simple – and I am sure someone must have pointed it out to Roger. The type of boxes he uses do not have a collapsible membrane and only let cider out when they let air in – thus bringing on the acetification.

The Full Moon is quite near to our Old Mill office in Wells where I am head of marketing and a frequent Friday lunch time venue for me. Through the year The Full Moon has a variety of other bag in box ciders. Usually sourced through particular wholesalers and of rather variable provenance. But it is good to offer variety. The first box of Stone's they had in early 2016 went down well and he has says he will order another in the near future. A locals' pub worth a visit if in Wells.

Stop press. 18th April 2016. The Rest and Welcome, Melbury Osmond, a delightful roadside pub on the A37 six miles south of Yeovil has just had a box of our cider.

That completes the survey of pubs that do Stone's cider. It is great that in this part of Somerset there is now a growing choice of pubs where you find good cider and the atmosphere to match. I do not intend to do a roll call – many other will appear in the body of the text. One I would just like to mention is the Cross Keys at Lydford – only about four miles down the road from the Travellers Rest. Tom the manager runs an excellent pub with plenty going on. He has a good and changing range of real ales and ciders. He usually has the excellent Harry's Cider from Long Sutton and one or two others. Tom is talking of trying to organise a Cider festival in Sept 2016 so I might see if he would like a box of our cider then.

Wassail – the blessing of the orchard.

It still takes me aback that when talking to people about 'doing' a wassail most people still do not have the foggiest idea what I am talking about. The West Country, just after Christmas, has in the past five or six years seen a huge proliferation of wassails being held. You now see accounts of them all over the country, in villages and in cities – especially where there are a group of apple trees. Community orchards are popular locations. However, even those who have heard of them and maybe even attended one seem to have very little understanding of what they are about. They get good coverage in the local press – they are very colourful and photogenic. A couple of years ago I read a feature in the Western Daily Press by journalist Simon Russell who has strong ties to the cider industry but his account about the 'pagan festival' had very little connection to the real history. I wrote an article for him – but I don't think he ever used it.

It is a shame that the press do not seem to want to know more rational information about wassail as the story is very interesting and the tradition goes back many hundreds of years. What makes this even more complicated is that there is no right and wrong about wassail. There are many different wassail traditions around the country and as will be seen it is constantly evolving.

My biggest bugbear is those who talk about it as a 'pagan tradition' and imply it has been happening as it happens now since pagan times. They bring in elements of a vast number of varied English country traditions – which really come from separate though equally interesting roots.

So what is wassail? In recent years I have been leading two wassail ceremonies. One for the Mid Somerset Show in the village of North Wootton and the other for Brue Valley Rotary in the village of Yarlington. With the responsibility of informing the public at these ceremonies I have made a quite extensive study of the subject and read everything I can find.

Without pretending to do an academic study I will outline the origins and describe the ceremony we carry out each year.

'Wassail' – 'good health' – the etymology of the word can be traced back in slightly different forms to both Saxon and Viking times. The first wassails would appear to be the passing round the banquet table of a steaming bowl of a hot alcoholic drink and each person taking a sip and shouting wassail. That drink may have been cider but it is far more likely to have been ale – perhaps fortified with spirit or one of our ancient drinks like Lambswool, Noggin or Mead. There would appear to be written records of this sort of wassail from as early as the 11th Century – a pretty old custom.

An evolution of this type of wassail, again probably originally dating back to medieval times, is what has been referred to as the 'Visiting Wassail' where a steaming bowl of drink was taken around the important houses of the area by a group of villagers being refilled by householders on route. This type of Wassail strikes one as less likely to have developed much before the decline of serfdom in the 14th and 15th century. It has had a long history though. When you read about ancient customs it is interesting to see how their popularity ebbs and flows. There was a definite boom of customs and traditions in the 14th and 15th century. The late 17th and early 18th century seems to have seen another such period. Then the late Victorians and through to about the 1920s seems to have seen a real blossoming and setting down of customs – much of what we see as traditional upon examination would seem to have been 'created' in this period. Created is definitely too strong a word. It is more that people who had a fascination with our rural past pulled together lots of strands of existing bits and pieces around the country and with them picked up some echoes of things of pagan origin and spun then into a semi coherent whole which probably bears little resemblance to the reality of the past. Probably the most extreme example of this process is the whole religion of Druidism and mistletoe. This seems to have been developed in the 19th century from a single short Roman reference and a lot of grasping at other strands.

For most of the 20th century many of these traditions were ignored but into the 21st century we seem to be having another sustained period of popularity and a further evolution. The fantastic books 'Stations of the Sun' by Ronald Hutton and 'Wassailing the British Midwinter Blessing Custom' by Simon Reed give the most coherent accounts of these developments.

The visiting wassail still exists in some occasional villages – though I expect most of these are actually of Victorian revivals. In the 17th century they seem to have become the property of local lads – or apprentices as they are sometimes referred to. They were a chance for semi acceptable boisterous behaviour and dinking – and a bit of begging for money from the 'big' houses as well. There are elements of this which have been carried into the wassails we know today.

The wassails we know today are the 'Orchard Wassails'. These owe just as much to a parallel strand of winter customs known as crop blessings. There a number of strong traditions around crop blessings. The legends of going to see the farm animals on Christmas Eve, on which night the animals can talk possibly spring from this. In the church the beginning of January sees Plough Monday when the farmers bought their ploughs to church to be blessed. Other crop blessings can be identified at this crucial time when the days have just started to get longer whilst food is getting shorter and people superstitiously want to do something to hope that the coming years is going to bring a bountiful harvest.

For orchard wassails the records do not go back anywhere near as far as with the other forms. The earliest is not until 1585 when the Tudor Dynasty was drawing to the end of its reign. The expert historians identify that there were scattered references to this over the next 50 years and use the spread to suggest that the tradition may have dated from either the late 15th Century or early 16th century.

The reason for this late start to the custom is relatively obvious, though it has been missed by most of those proclaiming pagan origins. There were scarcely any apple trees in England, let alone orchards, in the earlier period. Speculation has the first orchards being planted in a religious house in Dorset just before the Norman Conquest. Orchards and indeed cider seems to have been on a very limited scale mainly within religious institutions until well into the 14th or even 15th century until the 'liberating' of the economy with the gradual breakdown of feudalism. This was followed in the early 16th century by Henry the VIII's dissolution of the monasteries. It is important not to generalise but religious institutions are probably not the most fertile ground for the blossoming of pagan ceremonies. The orchard blessing therefore is of relatively late origin and its evolution comes from the 15th or 16th century. The increasing popularity of cider was a very gradual affair. Wine and ale were definitely the more prevalent drinks with a certain class divide. It was not until wine supplies were marginally under threat in the 17th century that cider had anything more than a small minority appeal and it is not until the 18th Century that it starts to become the farm labourer's drink on a wider scale and then mainly in the West of England. Indeed my researches in Devon backed by the more widespread research of my son Richie would suggest that much of the growth and commercialisation of cider came from producing a product that was largely exported to London where is was used by unscrupulous wine merchants who added sugars and sold as cheap wines.

The Wassail Ceremony

The two wassails that I lead follow a format that seems to be the main modern version of the event – though there are many variations. It seems to be based on the Carhampton Wassail – possibly the last remaining wassail in England in the 1950s and 60s which was picked up by the Taunton Cider Company to become an annual hospitality and publicity event to provide a heritage background to their marketing. This was then taken up by Gaymers and has been held in recent years at the Stewely Orchards until the problems C&C brands were having led to the sale of the orchards and its cancellation in 2015,

The ceremony is supposed to be traditionally held on Old Twelfth Night – the 17th January. Some people hold it on twelfth night – the 6th January but the legend is that the date was not changed when the calendar was changed in the 18th Century. Cynics such as myself may suggest that the date was fixed more to separate it from Christmas. There is little doubt that wassail is basically an excuse for having some fun on the dark evenings. With the revival in the past decade the date has become much more flexible – especially with the fixation of doing things at weekends. I know of Wassails on the 6th of January. In 2015 I attended Wassails on January 14th, 16, 17, and 23rd and as I write have one pencilled in my diary for 8th February!

The key feature is that you wassail an apple tree. Preferably the biggest or oldest one in the orchard. I have found that expediency and muddy ground these days usually results in the apple tree selected being one of the nearest to the gate which people can get around. For the second wassail we held in North Wootton we went back to the conveniently locate tree we had blessed the year before only to discover it had succumbed to mistletoe during the year and had been taken down. Note – do not consider the Orchard Wassail blessing as a cast iron guarantee of good crops for the next year!

A princess or queen is selected to carry out the blessing. At the Yarlington Brue Valley Rotary wassail the princess is selected in advance from the daughters of the Rotary members. Though given the age group in Rotary it is more likely to be a granddaughter – if Shepton Rotary were to use this method it could very well be a great granddaughter! At North Wootton for the Mid Somerset Show Wassail a crown has been woven from greenery and the first girl who arrives is asked if she would like to be the queen. This has proved a remarkably successful method, with the enthusiastic participation of those selected. The order of the next events is not always followed but they make up the essential elements of most wassails. Cider is poured into a large cider mug or a chamber pot makes a good alternative. A couple of bits of toast are dipped into the cider and the princess climbs a suitably positioned ladder to place the toast in the apple tree. This is part of the thanking the tree and giving something back in the blessing though people also suggest it is to encourage robins into the trees to eat unwanted grubs. Nice thought and I have used it myself but I am not at all convinced as to any historical origin as a motive behind this.

The key part of the blessing is the princess pouring the hot cider as a libation on the ground around the roots of the tree. This more clearly stands out as a giving something back and hoping for a good coming harvest as part of the blessing. The cider that is left in the pot is then passed around the watching crowd for everyone to have a sip and to share in the blessing. With modern health and safety I am not sure how many people really enjoy that part these days, though every wassail worth its sorts has some mulled cider!

We then sing the Wassail Carol. I have been to wassails where they try to come up with traditional local versions of the carol which are frankly unsingable except by folk singing specialists. I would rather listen to these, if we have to, and get the audience singing a rousing version of the Carhampton Wassail. To the tune of the nursery rhyme Miller of Dee

'Old Apple Tree. We wassail thee and hoping you will bear

For the lord does know where we will be till apples come another year

For to blo' (bloom) well and to bear well, merry let us be

And take off our hats and shout to the old apple tree.

Shouted

Old Apple Tree we wassail the and hoping thou will bear

Hats full, Caps full, three bushel bags full and a little heap under the stairs.

Usually we go for a rehearsal and as the first effort is always pathetic we have a second run through. By then people are in to the spirit of it and may know some of the words (we provide song sheets but they are difficult to read in a dark, often rainy orchard) and then we really let rip.

At the end of the ceremony everybody makes a big noise banging saucepans or similar and someone fires a shotgun through the branches of the tree. At North Wootton we are lucky to have Wessex Purchase who fires an old flintlock so there is a nice trace of sparks – at many others it is an ordinary shotgun which makes a noise but people usually miss it as it is not visual and they do it two or three times.

There is a quite a bit of controversy around the meaning of the noise and firing a gun. The popular status quo is that it is to drive the evil spirits out of the tree. The wassail historians are not so sure that it is part of the blessing. They think this is something added to the ceremony from the boisterous efforts of the local lads and apprentices and more allied to the riotous behaviour that has spilled over from the evolution of the Visiting Wassail. I am not sure it matters – it is great fun and the ceremony would be a bit drab without it.

That is really the core of a wassail and from the 18th century accounts most of those element would seem to have been there from the start. Especially from the late 19th century and in the past decade a number of elements seem to have been added.

Most prominent at many wassails is the bonfire – the North Wootton one is spectacular. There is a separate tradition in Herefordshire of lighting a circle of small bonfires which a part of a very different orchard crop blessings. Bonfires seem to have been added to the Orchard Wassail relatively recently. However it is a reflection of many fire and light traditions of varied sorts that run through the winter from fireworks night, though yule logs and others. Maybe something to do with encouraging the sun to return. These have a very long tradition, far longer than the presence of orchards, and have a much wider interpretation than being part of wassail. With these you can maybe see the shadows of pagan ceremonies. And they are great fun, we all love getting one side of our body toasted stood gazing into the flames – well I know I do!

Another folklore tradition appended to wassail is mummers. The stylized mummer plays also predate wassails and around here we are very fortunate to have the Langport Mummers who perform in pubs and events throughout the year. They are great fun and although sticking to the mummer play formula always add in modern references to political matters. Many unwary Landlords think it is a bargain that they don't charge to perform. They just want to have cider during the evening. It is quite surprising how much cider the troop can consume!

Another troop that turns out at many wassails are morris dancers together with their bells and sticks and endearing prat like appearance. Morris in some forms again predates the orchard Wassail, at first it was a court dance and then a dance of the aristocracy before it became a popular dance in the 17th century. It has had many ups and downs since then. What we know today really seems to date from the last couple of decades of the 19th Century and is associated with the folk movement of Cecil Sharp and the gathering of folk songs. In the early years of the 20th century it became very much associated with the rather misogynist tendencies of fascist sympathisers in this county, the leather trousers and buttock slapping rather give this way, but is has grown through this and there are now many female performers and indeed troops. These are people who are combining fitness activity with a love of folklore and are very welcome at wassails but have no direct relationship to the traditions.

At Yarlington we start with a different song; The Yarlington Wassail. Most wassail carols seem to have a common theme which suggests they all date from the spread of the popular printed word probably in the early 18th century which have then been adapted or evolved into local variations. The Yarlington Wassail song though is very different with a complex tune which makes it far more suitable for preforming rather than community singing. It would appear to date from the 1930s and is unique in that it actually talks about the growing of the apples and the seasons they go through. It is interesting to listen to and power to the elbow of the local folk enthusiasts who have hunted it out and have managed to get it performed in the village of its origin.

At North Wootton after the rain bespattered ceremony in the orchard we make out way into the tiny village hall where somehow everybody is crammed in for the mummer play, clog dancers and a local group of folk musicians. Later in the evening everyone is encouraged to dance but the rather bouncy hall floor is a concern! A ploughman's supper is served during the evening and the bar has a section of local ciders. This usually includes some of my Stone's bittersweet, some from popular local cider legend Roger Wilkins, some from a local farmer Edna Coombes which can be rather challenging to those not used to real farmhouse cider! And some commercial cider from the local Shepton Cider Mill.

It is all great fun and most people are eager to attend every year. To me this is one of the important events for 'finding good cider'. It is about the atmosphere, the fun and the linking into our heritage that make this and other wassails so important.

Sweet Alford

January 2015

One of the delights of our cider making is the cross over between trying to be proper cider maker and being experimental hobby cider makers. Although it may rather slow us down we try to do a few interesting experiments each year. Keeved cider has become regular and has won prizes in major competitions and we really like some of the hedgerow ciders we try – elderberry especially which as we cannot sell it (it being a made wine and needing to pay duty) we regularly drink at home in the evenings out of choice.

In 2013 Martin Berkeley of Pilton cider invited us to come and select some apples from a heritage orchard he has access too. Planted by Frances Showering, the legendary inventor of Babycham - it is in the grounds of his former mansion, Princes Lodge, on the hillside above the Shepton Cider Mill. In it there are two trees each of 88 different varieties of cider apples in a steeply sloping bush orchard which is now at maturity. It is now owned by a Russian billionaire and the site is surrounded by high walls topped with barbed wire and can only be entered through very solid security gate.

Martin has somehow got permission to pick up the apples and one Saturday morning he invited Richie and me to go and select a few apples to try making some single variety ciders. It was a mellow autumn morning and the steep slope made it very hard work. We wanted to select some sweet varieties of apple. We were side-tracked by selecting some very nice shiny red Stars of Jerusalem apples, a bittersweet variety where if you cut the apple in half there is a circle of 10 stars in the flesh. It looked nice but fermented out to a very harsh dry cider.

We moved on to Sweet Coppin, Taylors Sweet and Sweet Alford. We know that sweet apples do not make sweet ciders – they all ferment out dry. However, we were keen to see what arrived with low acid combined with low tannins. Apart from the very early Morgan Sweet which makes a pleasant light fresh cider which is slightly on the thin side but can be ready in time for Christmas we had no experience.

We kept them as three separate single varieties – basically a demijohn (5 litres) of each. We left these to ferment – though to be honest could not see much sign of activity. In the late winter we discovered some of them had developed a think silvery blue layer of some sort of mould. This could just be lifted off as a skin and where we dropped it in the garden took a fair time to degrade. Testing suggested the fermentation was very slow and there was still a long way to go.

As is the habit with demijohns they tend to get pushed to the back of the work bench and forgotten. No more moulds developed though they obviously had quite a deposit of lees. I wracked them off the lees once but as they were no way finished I left them to get on with it.

In January, looking for something to drink I spotted one of the demijohns and bought it in for Richie and I to drink in the evening. I confess to not taking the scientific approach and testing the sugars etc. We syphoned it off into a clean demijohn and poured our first glass. It was the Sweet Alford and it was absolute nectar. There was still a strong element of residual sweetness where it had not fully fermented out but it had also developed a rich mellow and complex flavour. The sort of cider you would love to be able to replicate in quantity but never can. It may have been a sweet cider but this was the natural sweet without any added sugar of sweetener which has a far superior taste.

Where did the success come from? Basically nature and probably temperature during fermentation. It had been made quite late in the season when temperatures were already dropping. I am pretty sure we made it without adding yeast, the lack of flocculation would strongly suggest this, so fermentation was likely to be slow getting going. In our garden shed the temperatures quickly drops, especially for small quantities of liquid in 5 litre demijohns. The fermentation must have 'stuck'. This is a very imprecise description of what happens when a fermentation appears to stop, or carries on very slowly. Sometimes this is because of a 'cold shock' which kills out a lot of the yeast. This can be induced by running the juice through a chiller – but we do not have that sort of equipment. Probably the most valuable element was time – at least 15 month from when it was started.

A wonderful cider like this is the sort of delight that is always very welcome to find for the 'hobby' side of our cider making.

The Salutation. Ham Green, Berkeley.

For Richie's birthday in late January we had had a very enjoyable family day at the Wildfowl Centre at Slimbridge in South Gloucestershire on the banks of the River Severn. It is a great place to go and we were delighted for the first time to spot Cranes in the wild – even though these Cranes were part of a project only a few miles from us in Somerset which had flown to the adjoining county. We have still yet to spot the cranes in Somerset!

Being the sort of person who always has an eye on how we can enhance a day out I had noticed many reports on social media about a pub called The Salutation which had recently won the CAMRA pub of the year. A high accolade indeed and as it was very close to our route home a visit was imperative.

There is always a worry as to what we are going to find on these visits to pubs we do not know. She regards the CAMRA Good Beer guide with a lot of suspicion and given some of the pubs we have ended up in at times I can't blame her. She therefore had doubts about this one. Would it be open at 4 o'clock on a Sunday afternoon? Would it be one of those local's pubs where visitors were frowned upon?

We found it a just out of the grounds of Berkeley Castle. It looked quite small and the car park was not tarmaced, a very traditional looking pub. We went into a pretty crowded bar were we looked around trying to work out the form. Very friendly customers pointed out to us that there was a table in the next room and we went through and made ourselves at home.

The selection of real beers and ciders was quite exceptional. I think there were four different ciders from Oliver's Cider in Herefordshire and a perry, a producer who you will be meeting again in these pages. There was also Wilkins cider from Somerset and a local Gloucestershire cider and a perry from Barnes and Adams which I had not come across before. Of course I tasted a pint of this and it was okay, but nothing as good as the ciders from Oliver's. Checking their web site it had an impressive amount about heritage and quality – but I am always a mite suspicious when it does not tell you exactly where they are based!

Anyway The Salutation was excellent for this cold winter afternoon. As well as the cider there was a good range of beers for James. You can see why it won the

CAMRA Pub of the Year Award. Even down to the effusive goodbyes and see you again soon when we left.

It may not have been soon but we did make another visit on another northerly family birthday day out – the excellent Sudbury Castle in June. The weather contrast was extreme and we joined the crowds sat out in the garden. We met Peter Tilley and his wife Claire. A young couple who had no experience in pubs other than as customers when they took over only a couple of years ago. I often find that it is the novices to the trade who set up the best pubs. They know what they want and have no preconceptions of what has to be.

On this visit we were lucky to find that the pub had just launched its own microbrewery 'Tilley's' and were serving its first brew, a very nice Porter. If asked what was my favourite type of beer I would usually go for a good Porter – and this was one. I of course had to have some Oliver's cider as well. Peter seemed to be an excellent chap and told us some of his plans – these seemed to have come to fruition when we made out next visit early in 2016.

There are holding a series of brew weekends when they invite the brewers from artisan breweries up to brew a beer there on the spot. They also have a cider evening with Tom Oliver matching ciders to foods, and most exciting of all they have a project Ham from Ham where they are using the meat from their home grown Gloucester Old Spot pigs. Do check their website to see what is going on.

Basically this is one excellent pub and well worth while having a place in this 'finding good' cider odyssey!

Early Doors Cider and Ale Bar

The first Sunday of February and for an afternoon drink I get the urge to try somewhere different. Although it is a bit of a drive around we go to the Early Doors Cider and Ale Bar at Draycott on the road to Cheddar. It has been open for about 18 months but I have never passed at the right sort of time and it had not looked that tempting.

It certainly looks unusual. A metal clad industrial looking shed that used to hold a fruit stall / shop selling strawberries and vegetables. And from the outside it looks quite small. Actually when we stepped inside it was a very welcoming small bar with plenty of people sat on the limited number of tables. We did wonder about the slightly unusual aroma but that was just because a dog had managed to wag its tail briefly into the log burner that was manfully trying to heat the shed in the intense cold. In fact on an artic exploration to the loo I discovered a very pleasant looking lounge bar area out the back- but unheated and far too cold for today.

Despite it being a relatively new enterprise there were plenty of locals at the bar and around, many quite happy to chat and offer advice on choice of drinks. 'Mine host' Jason was definitely a lively character which helped build a really good atmosphere.

Of course I had mainly come for the cider but after a bit of experiment settled on an excellent, newly tapped cask of Yeovil Ales Stargazer one of three real ales on a rack behind the bar.

There was a large range of ciders but as I later discussed with Jason I was a bit underwhelmed by the choice. For me a cider bar has the opportunity of supporting the many local artisan cider makers but here we had Somerset Tree Shaker and Somerset Snuffler, both from Shepton Cider Mills which although quite good ciders, I quite like the Snuffler, are made in the second biggest cider factory in the world in Shepton Mallet. Then there was Ashton Press from the Long Ashton Cider Company – which is in fact part of Butcombe Brewery and made by Thatchers cider – the third or fourth biggest cider maker in the country. Again not bad stuff at all – but hardly artisan, is this the right ethos? Though I certainly respect that anyone running a bar has to stock what they can sell.

There were local artisan ciders from Roger Wilkins, Rich's and Hecks. They are all good local farmhouse producers, but about the most predictable selection available. And unfortunately two out of these three were being served from the five gallon brown plastic barrels you see on the bar. The sad thing about these barrels is that to get the cider out you have to let air in. The cider often reacts to the air and begins to go off. After a week or so the cider can take on a distinct vinegary taste. I honestly believe the cider from this type of barrels on bars in pubs has done more to create a bad impression of farmhouse cider than any other single factor.

Especially as there is a great alternative in the modern 20 litre bag in box which lets no air gets into the cider so can last for months without deteriorating. We once forgot about a box of rather acidic Bramley Apple Cider we had made. When we rediscovered it after a couple of years it had matured nicely!

The Early Doors was a wonderful discovery, well worth going to for a drink. I had a decent pint of Hecks medium cider which was the one local farmhouse cider they had in bag in box. I intend to visit again soon to see Jason, enjoy the atmosphere and the drink!

Despite its being a bit off the beaten track for me I did go back three of four times during the year and was definitely not disappointed. Jason has taken on the running on a more permanent basis and has developed a very lively and unique bar. There is a touch of anarchy about the organisation, and on most visits there was something happening. Like trying to get the decorations up for a party starting in an hour's time or trying to get the food made for the next session and not having one essential ingredients so someone having to mind the bar whilst Jason dashes off to the supermarket in Cheddar.

Amazingly I think there was someone I knew in there each time I visited. The landlord of the excellent Queen Victoria in Priddy which is actually not that far away though on top of the Mendips probably 600 feet higher up. John Counsell, a local farmer who is a great character who I know through work at Old Mill and who I see on many of the agricultural shows throughout the year. Another time I went in on a Saturday afternoon and Mr Brian Stuart a former class master of my son James had just finished playing a set of blues music under the name of B Cooling. This is a place to meet people and everyone always falls into conversation with everyone else.

The range of cider has only marginally expanded. One time I went in and they had some cider from the excellent Wilcox cider which is made not many miles away in Shipham. In the autumn they had some excellent Worley's Harvest Moon however, although it was on the price list they had run out on my most recent mid-winter visit. Jason promised he would have it back in for my next visit. It was interesting looking at the selection following the news of the forthcoming shutting of the Shepton Cider Mill in July 2016. Somerset Tree Shaker and Snuffler were no longer available – I suspect they have been withdrawn. However it was interesting that two of the six draft ciders on offer also come out of the mill. Mole's Black Rat and Orchard Pig Hogfather. It will be interesting to see where production of these ends up.

Richie and I decided to drink the Wilkin's Dry and were very pleased with our choice. We stuck to the dry which must have been a relatively recent delivery and it was a fresh and excellent quaffing cider.

Living up to its reputation for something always going in the bar at Early Doors on this Saturday afternoon we saw a chap fixing acoustic panels on the wall above the door to try to overcome some complaints from neighbours over the noise from live music. Plus there were frantic attempts to get a small screen to pick up the rugby which some customers had arrived hoping to watch. Unfortunately the recent winds had damaged the aerial and despite a lot of fiddling no signal could be picked up – the customers seemed to be just as happy drinking cider and chatting. As an observation it was interesting to see that there were more pints of cider being drunk by women than men!

The combination of ciders and great atmosphere definitely make Early Doors a prime location for 'finding good cider'.

Yeovil Beer Festival – and cider too

Friday 21st of March and I was surprised and delighted to be asked along to a press photo shoot to help promote the Yeovil Beer Festival, to be held in early April, with an article in the Western Gazette. I thought I was invited as at Old Mill we are sponsoring a barrel again – however when I saw the select gathering I gathered it was because I write about cider.

It was a gorgeous sunny spring afternoon and we were at Harry's Cider in Long Sutton to be photographed clambering on straw bales in Harry Fry's newly planted orchard of Browns Apple. The Yeovil Beer festival is not organised by CAMRA but by the local Round Table to raise funds for local charities – a worthy effort. One of the key people behind it is Rob Sherwood the owner of the excellent Yeovil Ales, whose beers I am quite partial to. However he openly admits to not being a cider fan or knowing a lot about it. I met Russ from Funtasia and Simon from Mint Cabs who agreed to having a box of our Stones Bittersweet cider at the festival.

As well as a superb range of beers from all around the United Kingdom – they were delighted to be having the Welsh Champion Beer – they have a good range of local ciders. I was pleased to see that the selection of ciders did include some very good local 'real' or artisan ciders which was an improvement on a couple of years ago. However, as I discussed with them there was still an element of muddling.

If a festival is based on real ales, live and draft without carbonation, they should be reflecting a similar standard in cider. I genuinely think that although they understand real ale they are still not sure about comparable standards for an ethos of good cider. It is a complex issue about which I have written at length.

Here I can only try a brief summary of the key elements as I see it.
- There should be a strong connection between the cider maker and the apples – preferably it should be made of mainly cider varieties from West Country orchards. There is a surprising amount of cider from producers of all sizes that is made from imported concentrate from Europe or from dessert fruit.
- The cider should be slowly fermented at ambient temperature – not in a heated process.
- Unless it is being bottled (and not always then) it should not be micro filtered or pasteurised

- It should be made of near 100% apple, (or pear in the case of perry) juice
- The only additives should be sweeteners to taste and perhaps in some circumstances sulphite to ensure it meets health standards. Some purists would not like either of these but as cider ferments dry it would have a limited market with modern tastes.

These factors would exclude the ciders made in the most of the cider factories. Unfortunately as the factories make many brands for many people often purporting to be genuine farmhouse cider this is extremely confusing for the public – especially as many of them taste reasonable!

Talking to the organisers it became obvious that some of the ciders they are stocking would not fit the criteria – one in particular they were surprised at as they understood it was from a small farm based producer. This is one of my really big gripes. Marketing by larger producers who strongly suggest their rural roots and promote it as genuine 'real' artisan cider. I am not trying to outlaw or denigrate these products, I frequently drink them and recognise that some of them have a good taste. However, they are commercial products and I object to what is a deliberate policy of misleading the public and in doing so make it much harder for the genuine small producers to find a market for their traditional quality West Country cider products.

Anyway, the Yeovil Beer Festival has moved forward a lot in this area and all credit to this enthusiastic bunch for staging such a fantastic event!

Cider producers at Taste of West

February found me in my day job as Head of Marketing for Old Mill accountants and financial advisers, manning our stand at The Source, Taste of the West, Trade show at West Point Exeter.

Although some people are suggesting the cider revival may be slowing there was no sign of it here and the number of producers seems to be still growing. Old Favourites Sheppy's from Bradford on Tone were there with Mel their enthusiastic sales manager. Perry's from Dowlish Wake near Ilminster were back after missing a couple of years. The exuberant Barney Butterworth of Sandford Orchards was there again. I first met him at this exhibition about six or seven years ago when he was just getting going. They then had a very basic offering but now he has grown an excellent business and is one of the brightest of the new generation of cider makers. He is just moving into an old cider factory he has refurbished at Credy near Crediton.

There were some new names as well. Winkleigh Cider has been around for over 20 years, in part of the former Inch's cider factory in Winkleigh which was shut down shortly after being bought by Bulmer's in the 1990s. Former Cider maker David Bridgman kept it going but it has not travelled far from the very remote part of Devon around Winkleigh. This was their first time at a trade show and that is because the next generation has recently taken over, David's daughter Kylie and her husband Chris who is a great nephew of the original Sam Inch. I love it when there are these historical continuations. Obviously it is early days but there seems to be genuine enthusiasm and I look forward to seeing them again.

Another new exhibitor was Fowey Valley Cider from Cornwall. There are a growing number of cider businesses in Cornwall of a very mixed range of styles. This one only had its first batch of product ready to sell in the autumn of 2014 as they have gone down the 'champagne' cider route. Making a very high quality bottle conditioned cider in champagne bottles. It takes well over a year to make and is very labour intensive with daily bottle turning, freezing the bottle neck and expressing the sediment. I met the enthusiastic owner, Barrie Gibson, who has turned a cider making hobby into a business. He says the cider is made with dessert apples which can sometimes lead to a bland acidic cider – not in this case. The cider had an excellent fresh taste and it is good to see the development of some of these real quality products. He didn't need to show again in 2016 – he is comfortably selling all he can make!

The final new cider company exhibiting was Old Jollop from Ashgrove Farm Produce at Wedmore – real cider country in central Somerset. I had come across bottles of this last year. It is made by a group of friends of Toby and Lena Lee in the village. Jo Haggan was on the stand on the Wednesday and I discovered she knows my colleague Julia Banwell quite well. I knew something about the cider from Wessex Purchase who is another of the group of friends. He comes to fire the flintlock rifle through the trees at the Mid Somerset Show Wassail. It is a reasonable tasting traditional Somerset cider which they have bottled and gently carbonated. Apparently they have made 26,000 litres this year which will take some finding a market for!

For the sake of completeness I also spotted some other ciders on stands where cider was not the principle product. Luscombe Drinks make a very nice organic cider alongside their range of juice drinks. As do Heron Valley. Lyme Bay Winery have a few ciders as part of their range of fruit wines and liqueurs. Bays Brewery had a nice cider as part of their range of beers – made for them by Perry's.

Yes, there is a wide variety of excellent ciders out there for people to find.

Great Taste Awards – why so bland a choice of cider?

In late March I was honoured to again be a judge in the cider classes of the Great Taste Awards. These excellent awards are run by the Guild of Fine Foods and provide a platform for smaller artisan producers to show both the quality of their products and their innovation.

This worthy aim did not seem to quite come to fruition in the cider classes this year. There were six tables of judges each of whom judged 8 different ciders. The common feeling was that although there were some reasonable ciders there was very little that was outstanding. On the table I was on all the eight ciders were very drinkable. Two we didn't really reckon tasted of anything at all except the sweetener and the others were rather run of the mill. Bland, too sweet and safe. It is ironic that the best cider we tasted was one that included blackberry. It avoided the terrible pitfall of so many fruit ciders of having syrupy strong fruit concentrates overpowering everything else. I am sure a marketing man would describe it as 'subtle hints of blackberry' the only problem was that the hints were so subtle most of the judges could not taste them at all.

I was fortunate enough to judge again in 2016 shortly before completing this book. The same comments apply perhaps even more so. The entry was up – seven tables each with 12 ciders and again it was dominated by some rather bland and nondescript ciders. Nothing offensively bland but absolutely nothing to make you think 'wow'. Of the dozen our table tasted three were okay and one I may have bought again – however as we judge totally blind we do not know whose ciders we have tasted. The fruit ciders were on the whole the worst. Not merely because they had fruit in them. They were oversweet and because they are made wines were only 4% ABV – this need not be a bad thing but the taste of cider had disappeared totally. This was not the case in one cider flavoured with the herb meadow Sweet. I admit I had no idea what the herb meadowsweet should taste like – and still do not. Apart from having a very slightly dirty back taste this just tasted like a rather thin but attractively fizzy light cider.

I suspect that some of the issue comes from who is and isn't attracted to pay to enter this competition. I definitely got the impression that the hard core of established West Country cider makers had not entered. This is a shame. The Great Taste Awards gain a huge amount of publicity and the ability to put the sticker on bottles has in the past been well used. On the next day I again judged the bottled beer class where there were twice as many entries. There were very few disappointing ones and most were good to excellent. Innovation was aimed at making the best beers possible in a variety of styles. Addition of fruits etc. was minimal and many of the beers ranging from 3.8 – 6.5% I would certainly buy a pint of if I knew what they were! The noble sacrifice of judging.

It would seem that the resurgence of cider over the past few years has led to a reduction of variety and 'over safe' cider to gain general appeal. Sweet and lacking in character fits most of the current crop of commercial ciders and it is a shame that many of the smaller artisan producers appear to have followed suit. Oh for a hint of sharpness and some real character! It was a hot room and something to refresh would have been nice – surely that is what cider should be about?

There are signs that some of the public are becoming a bit more discerning and here in the West Country there is a growing demand for drier ciders. At recent shows and festivals I have noticed an increasing demand for dry and talking to fellow judge Nick Poole this morning he is finding this in his sales across Dorset. And even more interesting the traditional idea of dry for men and sweet for women seems to have been blown out of the water. I was at the Yeovil Beer festival last week where cider was going down a storm and the number of women drinking pints of dry ciders surprised me.

Let's hope this coming summer sees a continuation of this trend – sweeteners are not the nicest of ingredients and cider naturally ferments down dry.

The frustrating thing about these awards is that this is only the first stage of the process. Although we spend a whole morning judging and tasting some the best ones are put forward to the next stage and we never find out what we have been drinking! Some ciders you can guess from the shape of the bottle or the fact that they have failed to cover the branding on the bottle top when they wrap paper around the label. Sometimes you can slip the cover up and have a peek. I know one of the food and drink journalists I was judging with did this for us on a regular basis – only after we had judged. A few times we were even able to identify some of the ciders by their taste.

All in all a very enjoyable way to spend a morning meeting with an interesting range of food journalists and people in the food trade who I do not regularly come across. Most had pretty good taste though were rather inexperienced about the particular merits of different types of cider.

Orchards – the heart of good cider

It is the last weekend of February. It is still rather chilly but the sun is shining and there is more than a hint of the coming of spring. I drive down a beautiful hidden valley between Castle Cary and Bruton with a profusion of snowdrops carpeting the verge along with a brave show of daffodils and early primroses.

I am visiting Mark and Alison Tilley at Bottom Farm Haspen. They have lived there for about 6 years and with Mark until recently in Afghanistan with the military it has been the very energetic Alison who has largely been driving their project forward.

As Alison shows me around I get some idea of one half of the project. The renovation of the farmyard and farm buildings. When they first moved in the photographs they took show the farm yard as being more akin to a traveller's camp with rubbish and dilapidated caravans everywhere and the farm buildings in a perilous state of collapse.

Most of the rubbish has now gone – though there are still some rather ugly concrete buildings earmarked for demolition and there will obviously be a landscaping phase. However the key old stone barns have now been imaginatively and skilfully turned into their family home. It was love at first site for Alison when she first came to look at it, and although she had been in theory looking for a cottage with 20 acres for a smallholding there was something about the idyllic setting of Bottom Farm that Alison just thought she had to have – and she fought hard to get.

As a smallholding, which is now 110 acres, it is still relatively low key. When I arrive a farm student is working a mini tractor in the large productive vegetable plot – Alison worried in case they had ploughed out her row of strawberry plants! They were also in the middle of lambing their small flock of about 20 ewes. But the main substance is two large cider apple orchards. One immediately opposite the entrance to the farm across the narrow lane. The other immediately to the side of the house. There are other orchards down the lane as this was part of the Haspen estate formerly owned by Henry Hobhouse.

These are mature bush orchards, probably planted in the 1980s or 90s. To my mind and eyes this is the most pleasing sort of orchard. Trees of a controlled size planted in neat rows with a herbage strip along the base of the trees which are planted about 15 feet apart. With good management, including regular pruning, spraying and feeding this type of orchard should produce between 15 and 25 tonnes a season. Before the Tilley's took over there had been a few years of neglect and yields had dropped but Alison took over the pruning and yields have started to go sharply back up. Last year they sent out over 700 tonnes of apples. Pruning is an ongoing work. Especially as the trees keep on growing and you can only prune a maximum of one third of the wood each year. There are many considerations – like stopping the trees getting too tall; stopping the branches getting too thick and keeping out the light; thinning the regrowth; getting out braches that are growing across the centre of the tree or in the wrong direction; cutting out branches that will tear away from the tree if they have a good crop; cutting out braches that are sticking out too far and will be awkward when harvesting the apples. Pruning is a mixture of knowledge and intuition which can only be gained with experience. Alison has been on a steep learning curve and the evidence is that she has got to grips with it really well.

This is the time of year when orchards look their neatest. The grass is short and the trees all look neat without the clutter of leaves. The question is always ' what is the crop going to be like this year' – a particularly relevant questions as in 2015 in the West Country in general the crop was so good that we are not expecting another quite that good. We inspect some of the branches and there appear to be a good number of the short spikes which are fattened where they meet the branch indicating fruit bud – the signs are reasonably promising.

These days bush orchard like these form the majority of the cider orchard landscape that you see as you drive around. Particularly up in Herefordshire in the area between Ledbury, Much Marcle and Leominster where it almost seems to be a monoculture. In Somerset they are more scattered but there are still many orchards around, they surround Julian Temperley's Burrow Hill in the South Petherton area. There are plenty here in the south east corner of Somerset. There is that wonderful area down through Melplash in Dorset. Perhaps the biggest plantings in recent years have been in North Somerset around Sandford where the Thatcher family have been responsible for extensive planting.

It is interesting to note that this is not a historic landscape in the usual sense of the word. Bush orchards only date from the 1970s when the larger scale cider mills discovered they wanted consistency and quality of crops. If you go back to the wonderful large scale Ordinance Survey maps of the 1870s you will see really extensive orchards marked, some Somerset Villages appearing to be nothing but orchard. This is a touch illusory. These were all the traditional orchards with only about 45 trees to the acre. These orchards would have been very much a part of the whole farming operations. The traditional picture is of sheep grazing them. They would also have been used for grazing cattle and my historian son Richie is finding evidence that they would also have been used for horticulture and in the days before large farm machinery indeed for arable cereal growing. The decline of the acreage under orchard is also rather misleading. These traditional orchards would only have normally yielded about 3 tonnes an acres so it would take about 6 acres to get the apples you would expect from one acre of modern bush orchard.

The legacy of these old style orchards is very apparent around Somerset. There are still hundreds of traditional orchards around. Most are in extremely poor condition. Missing trees that have fallen and not replaced, sometimes with old trees hanging on growing almost horizontally. The trees are often straggly and have an unkempt appearance as pruning has not been regularly carried out. I have been to orchards like this and struggled to find a dozen sacks full of apples to pick up at harvest time.

Even worse is that so many of them have been overrun by mistletoe. Most of the mistletoe in Somerset it not attractive. It grows in huge dirty yellow/green bunches that would not make a suitable decoration to hang up for Christmas frolics. In fact most of the mistletoe we hang up at Christmas is imported from France. The mistletoe growing in our traditional orchards is a parasite sapping strength and is slowly but surely killing the trees and it is practically impossible to control. You can prune out every year but unless you block out light from the wound for two or three years it will just grow back. There are sprays, but most of these are retardants which again do not provide a long term solution. Although there is joy at harvest time finding cider apples in long grass they are extremely difficult to pick up and I find these old orchards a bit depressing. A bit like nursing homes with an atmosphere of the inevitability of death and decline!

But back to brighter matters. By April and May the bush orchards will be covered with the wonderful apple blo' – the whites and pinks of blossom. One of the loveliest sights in the English countryside. You can see it driving around but even better is to get out of the car and walk in it. There are a number of orchards which open to the public for weekend events at this time of year. One of the biggest is The Big Apple Blossomtime around Pultney in Gloucestershire where there are a lot of things going on – including tasting the ciders that were made the previous autumn. Unfortunately I have been unable to get to this May Bank Holiday weekend event as I have other cider events going on in Somerset.

After blossom and fruit set the apples on the trees seem to disappear in the profusion of leaf growth. It is not until September and October that the apples reappear and there is the vison of red and green apples laden on the tree as they convert their starches to sugars to be ready for harvesting.

Local to me here in Somerset we have West Bradley Orchards run for the past 25 or so years by Edward Clifton Brown. We took Richie and James there from a very young age and every years go to the 'pick your own apples'. For Richie and me it is a sort of pilgrimage we never miss. Dessert apples you have picked yourself always taste vastly superior to anything you can get from the supermarket.

In most autumns the wet sets in whilst the apple harvest is being carried out and trying to get in and out of orchards in any vehicle, or even on foot if they are on a slope, becomes a treacherous battle with mud. Unless there is a dry spell when pruning can start orchards are then best avoided until the early spring like today. The exception is on the increasingly rare occasions when there is snow. The trees then take on a magical appearance which should not be missed! Of course we all do traipse into Orchards for the Wassail Ceremonies in January. A great fun part of the good cider experience – but as the orchards are then cold, muddy and dark it is perhaps not the best time to experience then for the joys of growing apples.

To experience orchards there are a good number of cider producers from Cornwall to Hereford who include an orchard trail in their offering to those coming to buy cider. These are often excellent to go for a short walk and are an ideal way of getting closer to nature, seeing wildlife and experiencing 'good cider'. They have a peacefulness about them which is wonderful to find in our hectic world.

Why are orchards so important for good cider?

Orchards are the source of all 'good cider' and West Country orchards are the essential source of all good West Country cider. 'Good cider' is all about the harvest of apples and the making of them into cider and the heritage and social activity around them. Cider made with apples from West Country cider orchards has a rich heritage and it is interesting that it is the large scale producers Westons, Thatchers, Bulmers and the former Shepton Cider Mill are the biggest cider apple growers and purchasers who are doing most to encourage the promotions of orchards and improve varieties. Cider makers who are reliant on the delivery of tanker loads of important concentrate need viewing with suspicion.

Back to the Tilley's at Bottom Farm. The reason for my visit was to settle up for an odd tonne of Dabinett apples I had at the very end of last autumn's harvest. I had been very keen to get some Dabinett into our blend – it makes a light clean cider. Cider is not just about the blend of sharps, bitter sharps, sweets and bittersweet it is also about the taste of the apples within that blend and Dabinett and Brown's would be two apples Richie and I are always keen on including. For some reason we had been a bit short of these during the season and we were keen on getting some and were delighted the Tilley's could help. These apples made some of our best cider

A long weekend in Shropshire – via Herefordshire

It was in April that we got away for a family long weekend in Shropshire. For the second year we rented a wonderful cottage at Squliver, near the marvellous pub at Bridges by the foot of the Long Mynd mountain and on the road leading up to the car park on the east side of the Stiperstones ridge. Just beautiful, with wonderful countryside, superb views, good wildlife and birds, some excellent historic buildings, good pubs with good food, some interesting local breweries and beers but rather limited impact with cider. This is something of a surprise as a bit of delving suggests that Shropshire has a fairly extensive history of cider orchards. The 1881 census shows it as having around 4,000 acres of orchard – similar to counties like Monmouth, Dorset and Cornwall which make a bit more of their cider heritage. I have visited one cider farm in the shadow of the Clee hills, as stark a bit of country as you can find. The cider was disappointing. Draft that was advanced in the process of turning acetic and a bottled cider that was okay to drink but compared with many superior bottles you wondered why anyone had gone to the trouble. I have also had a bottle of a very wine orientated cider from somewhere near the wonderful but rather foodie town of Ludlow. However, to get to Shropshire from the south you do so by driving through Hereford and that is a bit more pertinent to this book.

I had grown up loving Shropshire from the Lone Pine series of children's books by Malcolm Saville many of which are set on the Long Mynd and Stiperstones. For some reason which I cannot fathom I had never got around to visiting them. My parents had been hectored into taking me to many other Saville locations around the country along with the locations of the Arthur Ransome books. I had read these books to our boys when they were still relatively young but for some reason Shropshire had always been left off our agenda. I think it was about 15 years ago when the boys were both young teenagers that we went on a holiday to the black and white villages of north Herefordshire and on a couple of day trips we had started to explore the beautiful countryside of the south Shropshire hills and the border lands with Wales. I think we have returned to that part of Shropshire more years than we haven't ever since then including a couple of visits with the Malcolm Saville Society. And principally on the way to and from Shropshire I have gradually got to know a fair amount about Hereford cider.

On that first visit 15 years ago, before cider gained its current popularity I made a beeline to Dunkerton's Cider – which was not many miles from the village we stayed in. It was already then an excellent cider. I remember an attractive Hereford bull in the field near the farm and that you had to buy your cider with a demijohn to get a gallon. Quite expensive for the initial purchase but I did manage to make another trip to get it refilled during the week to get the unit cost down. This was at a time when the boys were taking their first tentative sips of cider. We also paid our first visit to the Cider Museum in Hereford itself and I read about the history of Bulmers Cider.

I suspect it was on our next trip up that we detoured via Weston's at Much Marcle. The first of three or four times I have taken the excellent cider tour of their works and bought product in their shop. One visit was for an evening outing of the Chartered Institute of Marketing and provided a very interesting insight to their products and aspirations. One thing I admire is their honesty for a national company. They are definitely in the top five nationally by volume along with Bulmers, Shepton, Thatchers and Aston Cider in Birmingham. The Weston's Brands are now quite well known and it could probably be suggested that they represent the respectable face of large scale cider production. The brands include the quality range of Henry Weston bottled ciders – at 8.3ABV some of the strongest readily available ciders. Their main Keg line is Stowford Press which is available in many pubs. There is Old Rosie, a strong cloudy cider which fools many with its drinkability. Then there is Wychwood, formally known as Weston's Organic which is an exceptional bottled cider. Although I like their bottled ciders and have had good experiences with their keg cider and cider on draft I must confess to frequently being disappointed by their cider when it is supplied bag in box. I have had this at various cider festivals and in many of the cider pubs in Bristol. I am just not at all sure why it should not match up to their usually high standards. At the Weston's cider mill you can go on a fascinating guided our around a modern cider mill which still retains many traditional aspects. They explain that they source apples locally – the mill is surrounded by miles of neatly planted bush orchards. One suspects mainly Michelin and Dabinett but proper cider apples anyway. They explain that for space reasons and to keep producing the whole year around that they concentrate their own juice. They ferment this up to a strength of 14% which they then use as the base to dilute down to their range of products. Cider purists will frown at this – and according to CAMRA it means it cannot be considered 'real' cider whatever that means. You will have noticed that it is a phrase I keep clear of. The tour ends with a tasting of some of their excellent products and a chance to buy cider in their shop. I can certainly recommend it for all cider fans and would suggest that those who have a rather narrow preconceived idea of what makes good cider should go, listen and see with an open mind.

Other cider makers who I have broken my trips to Hereford by visiting include Gwatkin's Cider at Abbey Dore in the Golden Valley to the West of the county. This is in an area of rolling farmyard and Gwatkin's is certainly situated on a working farm. I know on my visit the main centre of attention was moving cattle rather than serving in their slightly out of character modern small farm shop building. Nothing wrong with putting the farming first. Dennis Gwatkin with his broad face, rustic appearance and bushy beard is one of the characters of the cider scene. He makes a lot of single variety ciders and I particularly liked the dry Foxwhelp.

Even further west Richie and I on one trip stumbled on the Orgasmic Cider Company where we were served by a young girl student. Apparently the family who own the farm are big apple growers who supply Bulmers and Weston's but thought they should have a go at making cider themselves.

Near Leominster is Newton Court Cider. Although I didn't go there on this trip I have been there a number of times before. During the year I bumped into Paul both at the Bath and West Show where he was visiting and amazingly at the BBC good food show at the NEC. I was at this show to judge cheese in the Guild of Fine Foods World cheese championship. This was, to put it mildly, an interesting experience – particularly as the vast majority of the cheeses appeared to be sheep, goat or strange soft cheeses from around the world. I did have some cheddar but not much.

Both times I met Paul he was with Moria who is working on the marketing with him for three days a week. When I first knew Moira she was working for the Somerset Chamber of Commerce so I had a fair bit to do with her in the past but now with her husband has set up a 'glamping' enterprise nearby in Herefordshire. Moria is an expert on social media and a great friend of my colleague Kim who looks after this at Old Mill.

Early in April 2016 I did a similar short break to Shropshire and did manage to drop in to see Paul and Moria thanks to appointments made on Twitter! Newton Court cider is across the fields from the big Cadbury's factory a couple of miles south of Leominster. I was with Richie as well as Christine and James. Paul gave us tastes of some perry out of oak barrels to drink – very nice it was - and an extremely nice dry cider from last autumn made from apples from a Marchers Cyder Circle stalwart Roger Melpass. Very nice it was too – the type of cider you like to find. We also tasted a bottle of a Foxwhelp cider which had stopped during fermentation and been bottled to give a good level of residual sweetness – which combined with the high tannin and high acid of the Foxwhelp apple made an extremely pleasant and interesting cider.

Newton Court Cider is a 150 acre organic farm set with a wonderful traditional farmyard. There are Hereford suckler cows – we helped move one out of the vegetable patch – sheep and 15 acres of orchard of mixed perry and cider fruit. They are now making approaching 70,000 litres of cider and have developed a number of brands for the smaller 330ml bottles, like Panting Partridge Perry and Gasping Goose Cider. It is certainly somewhere well worth dropping in to.

I have also been to the Tiger Orchard of Simon Day who runs Once Upon a Tree. Simon is a fascinating and innovative cider maker who I once had the honour of judging the single variety classes of cider with at the Bath and West Show. He has been the leading exponent of trying Ice Ciders in this country. This originates in Canada where cider is sometimes made with frozen apples. Here you are more likely to freeze the juice immediately after pressing and as it melts collect the thick juice that defrosts first. You end up with some juice that is much higher in sugars than normal juice – you have in fact naturally concentrated it. If you try to do a conventional fermentation with wild or normal cider yeasts they run out of steam and leave a cider that has very high levels of residual sugars. Richie and I have experimented with it and come up with some excellent results. However they have not been consistent and we have had problems with the product developing strange tastes in the bottle over time. No doubt we will try again in the future but it takes a lot of effort – not the least transferring to the freezer of an Ice cream making friend for a couple of days! Simon seems to have perfected the art – however it is an expensive produce to produce and commands a very high price tag. If describing the product to people I tend to say it is like a sweet dessert wine.

Three of four years ago Simon and his wife set up the Three Counties Cider shop on the high street in Ledbury. This was our first port of call for this long weekend – stocking up. I say first port of call, on reflection it was the second as we had stopped for the loos at the Gloucester Services on the M5. If motorway services are not somewhere you would think of visiting then think again. The Gloucester services are run on a totally different basis and the central part is totally based around an up market farm shop focused exclusively on local artisan food producers. There is an excellent range of ciders in bottles on offer including some producers I had not come across before – the only criticism would be the usual one for motorway services – the goods are more expensive than elsewhere.

The Three Counties Cider shop is minute but has an excellent range of bottle ciders from across the three counties. Simon's 'Once upon a Tree' ciders are to the fore but there is fair representation from other producers. He also has two or three ciders on draught to buy to take away in containers. It being the three counties there is also an excellent selection of Perry's on offer as well. The cider shop model is an interesting one. It is something I am always tempted have a punt at – but until I have paid off my mortgage I just can't afford to take a punt at it.

We pick quite a few bottles from producers we know we are not going to see on this trip and get both a cider and a perry on draught. It is an interesting generalisation that the price is higher In Hereford than you tend to find similar ciders in Somerset or Devon. I think that this is because most Three Counties producers are new producers and they are part of a wider foodie movement who have the confidence to charge for quality. In Somerset there is still a mentality which expects cider to be the cheap farm workers drink.

We progress on to Oliver's Cider & Perry. It is Saturday morning which is just about the only time this open to the public except for prearranged parties. Tom Oliver is legendary in the cider and perry world and this is just before he won his award for contribution to cider at the Bath and West. Although this is my third visit it is the first time that I have been there when Tom is there. He is often overseas – raising the flag of West Country cider and perry in the US. Plus of course cider is far from the only string to his bow. He is also well known in the music industry and especially as the tour manager for the excellent Scottish duo the Proclaimers.

However, the lack of Tom is not the draw back you might think. He has Yarrick, a farm and cider manager who is eastern European but manages to speak good enough English to talk you through the ins and outs of making cider with Tom.

He shares a bank of knowledge and the enthusiasm with which he speaks about some of the innovative products they are experimenting with showing him to be a genuine port of call in his own right when 'finding good cider.' On our last visit Tom had been at a food fair in Ludlow – but this time we strike it lucky and have a good chat with Tom. Although he has a reputation for being one of the greatest cider makers he is very much part of the wider cider fraternity and talks with Richie and I as fellow cider makers. Though I am sure we learnt more from him than he did from us!

One part of the conversation which fascinated me was his suggestion that it is the women who go for the dry ciders. He thinks this comes from drinking dry white wine and he suggests that when they have hen nights it is the dry ciders that they all go for. As a dry cider fan myself I think this is very encouraging and my observations throughout the rest of the year tend to have confirmed this impression – though if you mention it to many of the cider makers in Somerset they think you are mad and believe that for women the only thing they will go for is ultra-sweet. I think they may be missing a trick – there is a need for cider makers to promote good dry ciders and to offer quality alternatives to over sweet drinks.

The same message was repeated on our trip back after the weekend when we managed to quickly drop in at Ross on Wye Cider. Mike Johnson runs Ross on Wye cider which until very recently was based at Broome Farm. I had had one of my best ever 'finding good cider' sessions on the farm a few years before when Mike gave a fascinating talk and demonstration to a party from east London who learnt how you could come up with totally different ciders by blending ciders with different attributes in terms of tannin in particular but also acid and sweetness. However although the cider is still made at the farm Mike has now bought The Yew Tree public house up the hill on the main road at Peterstow. He had not been in the pub that long and until the week I called their cider shop had been in a room behind the bar. However, that week he had opened his new cider shop in a new building out the back. Heaven, with four 1,000 litre bag in boxes. One of a perry and three different dry blends.

Unfortunately we had not scheduled long for a stop so had to move on. Mike and Ross on Wye cider also do a fantastic range of single variety ciders of interesting named variety blends in either 500ml bottles or in 75cl for a still product. We hastily bought a selection to take home with us – yes we had just about drunk all the ciders we bought on the outward journey for our long weekend. Fortunately Richie and I were to come back to The Yew Tree later in the year for a fantastic afternoon which you can read about later in this book.

There are more Hereford cider makers I have yet to visit – and of course there are a good number of cider producers in Worcestershire and Gloucestershire where I have not met so many – not to mention Monmouthshire. However, I have in front of me a recent copy of the tourist leaflet delineating the Hereford Cider Route. I think in this short section I have mentioned 9 out of 15 producers – so I have certainly made a good start.

Powerstock Cider Festival

One of the greatest events in the 'finding good cider' calendar is the Powerstock Cider Festival at the end of April. Around 500 people cram into a rather dated timber built village hall in the grounds of the local primary school in this very small village hidden down the lanes just to the north of Bridport.

This event is at the heart of the Dorset Cider revival and has over the past 15 or so years raised many pounds for charity and the local community. It feels strange to me sitting down to write about it again as my most recent book was about the Dorset Cider revival and Powerstock featured largely. However just in case there are a few of you who have not read the only book ever written on Dorset Cider a very brief recap.

Ten years ago if you had suggested to anyone that Dorset was a cider county with a long tradition they would have given you strange look and said the cider counties are Somerset, Devon and Hereford. I say 'read your Thomas Hardy'. He shows a rural county in the nineteenth century where cider is a real part of the farming way of life. Admittedly the tradition had nearly died out by around the turn of the millennium. But into the vacuum came local builder Nick Poole; very much centred around his activities in Powerstock and capitalising on the counties 'foodie' aspirations the Dorset Cider industry has been totally relaunched and with over 20 producers operating at least partially commercially is in a very healthy state.

The Powerstock Cider festival is very much the embodiment of this. Around 30 cider producers get together at lunch time for a hearty meal of something like sausages and mash. Just over half the producers are from Dorset and the rest from all around the country – I have come across a Cornish producer there, a sprinkling from Somerset and Devon, or even the eastern counties. There is usually a very strong contingent from the Three Counties, Hereford Gloucester and Worcester. Most are craft cider makers on the smaller scale and nearly all are people who live and breathe cider heritage. There is also representation from the 'cider sheds' which abound in this part of Dorset. Clubs of people who get together to make cider in the autumn and then drink it throughout the year. A great institution.

The ciders here are, to put it politely, variable. There are the local commercial producers and others, like myself, for whom it is only a bit more than a hobby and others which are from complete amateurs. Some ciders are over dry, some are close to being vinegar – others are real hidden treasures! The fun is in the finding out which.

In the afternoon the producers are supposed to taste each other's ciders and judge them against each other. Nick and his wife Dawn keep control but it usually becomes a bit of a scrum with far more people judging than there are producers present. I think they are tightening up this year on whose votes actually count! I know one year Richie and I were doing our tastings together and we set aside a lot of 'dry' ciders which tasted distinctly sweet. These qualify as dry because artificial course does not alter the specific gravity but should not be looking for in a dry cider. Needless to say with the public addiction to sweet tastes some of the sweet tasting drys won!

In 2015 there was a new class and along with Bob Chaplin I had been asked to judge it. Bottle conditioned ciders where a natural fizz is generated in the bottle. These ranged from wonderful crafted keeved cider to some ciders where a spoonful of sugar had been added a few weeks before and hadn't really had time to build up fizz. This competition broke with Powerstock tradition by having external judges – but of course with bottled product you can't really have 50 people getting a sample out of a small bottle.

The result of the bottle conditioned class was almost inevitable. Although it was a blind tasting one bottle of keeved cider stood way out above the others. West Milton Cider, from the neighbouring village, specialise in keeved cider and have even won at a French competition, the French being the masters of this style. And who is West Milton Cider – none other than Nick Poole! He is a quiet genuinely self-effacing chap and I think he was most embarrassed at winning. I suspect his motivation for starting the class was to encourage the development of premium ciders in Dorset and definitely not for self-glory! It will be interesting to see how the class develops.

The judging goes on most of the afternoon and it is just great to sit and chat with other cider producers and fanatics. A number of folk musicians are usually playing in the background and it is just a great atmosphere.

From about 6 o'clock the public arrive. This is where the charity aspect starts with all the cider producers donating a barrel of cider and the public buying strips of tickets to have tasters. The food stalls with burgers or pasties are very necessary to soak up surplus cider and a big crowd soon builds up, especially if it is raining and people want to cram inside. A band starts to play, for the past few years it was the Skimity Hitchers – the Dorset scrumpy and western band. I confess in the rather low ceilinged hall with such a crowd of people I found the noise a bit much but I had a good chance later in the year of hearing the Skimity's in more amenable surroundings!

This simple format works and a great time is had by all – there is always greater demand for tickets than there is space to accommodate them and thousands of pounds have been raised. A truly great 'finding good cider' event on every level that you can think of – cider, heritage, social, music and more!

Whilst down in Dorset it is perhaps time for me to give a brief summary of what can be found in the county. Having focused on it over recent years to research my book 'Dorset Cider' it may feature less than it deserves in other parts of this current book.

Powerstock is in a group of villages which perhaps represent the focus of Dorset cider. Powerstock and West Milton, Melplash, Symonsbury and Netherbury and the land around. If you go back to the smashing large scale OS maps published in the 1870s you will see that most of the land is covered with orchards. There are still some really excellent orchards in this area grown on a strip of soils which are particularly favourable. Just about three miles up the lane towards Melplash you past the excellent orchards of Rupert Best at Hinknowle. He has around 60 acres of cider orchard, mainly bush orchards with key cider varieties. Rupert is a professional grower and for many years supplied the Taunton Cider Company and this then switched to Gaymers in Shepton Mallet. His apples now go to a much wider range of people and in a good year he produces over 800 tonnes of apples. He is a big character in the cider scene and was responsible for the establishment of the marvellous Cider Marquee and competition at the Bath and West Show.

For many years his orchards were looked after by his manager Chris Vye but in the past couple of years, with Chris past retirement age, Mark Rogers has played an increasingly important part in managing them. Mark is a young and energetic participant in the cider scene. He makes both honey and cider. His cider is sometimes called 'Rogers' and sometimes called Twinways after the superb orchard that he is tenant of. He lives locally in Melplash with his young family. Mark is someone whose knowledge and judgment of cider is excellent and he uses different blends of apples to produce his different ciders along with different levels of back sweetening with pasteurised juice. The result is some very fresh drinkable ciders. Over the past few years he has put up buildings to allow him to produce on site and has a small education centre there. He is one of few producers I know who has actually cut down on his production levels. He has such a variety of interests that he does not want to be a busy fool producing high volume low margin cider especially after having one of his large wholesale customers do the dirty on him. Mark is fascinated by farm history and rural heritage. When we get into a conversation it always reverts to these welcome topics.

Nick and Dawn Poole are now West Milton Cider. After a decade of building up his cider production Nick gave up his building business in 2014 and went full time into cider. He sources many of his apples from Rupert Best and makes some excellent ciders. His speciality is keeved Cider, as mentioned above he has beaten the French at this. However it is the inclusion of some of the keeved ciders into his draught that makes his cider stand out. They attend a lot of local shows and festivals and along with other local producers their cider is likely to be found in The Stable – the pizza restaurant in Bridport.

A few miles to the west you come across the 15 acres of wonderful orchards of the Strong Family who trade under the name of Dorset Nectar. Oliver and Penny have done a fair amount of globetrotting before settling here. I think they are of English origin but have South African accents and spent time in the USA before arriving in Dorset. They have had a long battle to get planning permission for their bungalow in the orchard but after a few years the County Council planners have had to admit that the combination of Cider and free range eggs made a viable agricultural business. They have five children and I think four of them were present with them at Powerstock this year. Dante I know well – he works on producing cider and fabricating the equipment they use. The next son Ryan is more into the marketing aspects and has been studying for a history degree. He took the wonderful photograph that became the cover for my 'Dorset Cider' book. The Strong's make a wonderful range of ciders from the apples in their

61

orchard and they have spent a lot of time developing a range of 500ml bottled ciders with some fantastic labels.

Going slightly further afield – five miles up one of the most deserted lanes I know of due north from West Milton you come to Kingcombe where you find the Crocker Brothers. They were former Dorset farmers, indeed I had called on Paul when I was a feed rep with Dalgety. They both now have jobs away from the farm in the building trade and much of the farm is now fishing ponds. They make traditional cider from local orchards though are not looking to make a fulltime living from it. They have planted some trees of their own and have access to others but had not ended up making a large amount of cider in the autumn of 2014 because of shortage of the apple crop. They provide a couple of local pubs and some local events but it is not a cider that is available widely. They are always at Powerstock and they have a well-made traditional cider which varies from year to year as nature intends.

From the other end of Dorset – more up towards Salisbury and on to the chalk soil comes Cranborne Chase Cider. Bill Meaden is the young cider maker and his father Simon also is likely to be in company with him. They source apples from various Dorset orchards – including Simon Baxter of Long Burton south of Sherborne who also makes his own award winning cider under the name of Sherborne Cider. Cranborne Chase cider is from my experience always very drinkable and they get it out and about. Bill is also the Brewer at Sixpenny Handley Brewery and the cider is available in the Brewery Tap shop – along with some excellent beers! They usually hold one big cider event a year on their farm. One year they will do an event to support Farm Sunday, the next they will have an end of summer festival.

Bill's cousin is also likely to be at Powerstock. He is Tom Percy from West Orchard Farm on the Isle of Purbeck tucked away behind Corfe Castle. Another young farmer he has a lovely little set up producing local cider. Sometimes this is for sale at the local Square and Compass pub at Langton Maltravers. This is an institution with landlord Charlie Newman an occasional visitor to Powerstock. His family have been running the pub for generations and it is well worth a visit in its own right – let alone the fact that he makes a considerable amount of his own cider. You can always spot Charlie – he is the one wearing a beret and looking very much like a Frenchman.

Another pub in that area which is well worth a visit is The Castle at West Lulworth. The owner's son Alex – also sometimes met at Powerstock – stocks a very wide selection of ciders. He describes it as a permanent cider festival.

Dan Green is another visitor. He has a very nice orchard near Cattistock and is still earning his cider making. He has a cosmic element about his and his ciders have names like Stargazing. He also has a double decker bus fitted out for catering and can be found doing catering alongside his cider at a number of festivals.

My fellow judge for the Bottle Conditioned cider class at this year's festival was Bob Chaplin. After 40 years with Shepton Cider Mill and being the long serving secretary of SWECA the South West Cider Makers Association – Bob is now a Dorset Cider maker – working for Oliver Tant, a businessman, who has set up Copse House Cider in the north of the county. As you would expect of Bob he has used his expertise to produce some excellent ciders and they won the Bath and West at their first attempt. Their ciders are available in some local pubs in the Gillingham and Shaftesbury area and their excellent bottled ciders are available much more widely.

Another regular Powerstock attendee and frequent winner is the extremely competitive Martin Inman of Dorset Skipper cider. He is a former financial services salesman who is really passionate about his ciders which he makes not far from Wareham. The Dorset Skipper is a butterfly which makes a very attractive label and the clean, full complex tasting ciders are really good as well.

The first time I met Charlie Harris from Burton Bradstock was at Powerstock. He was only just starting then and I got his name wrong in my 'In Search of Cider' book. I wrote him up in much better detail in Dorset Cider and I understand that the huge potential of the farm and heritage museum he has inherited from his grandfather is now being capitalised on. He is young and energetic and is now getting his cider out and about. I have seen him advertising a big cider camping event later this year. The shop and visitor centre on his farm are now worth a visit.

In this brief roundup I should also mention the former Penny Whatmore of the Dorset Cider Museum at Overmoigne. I keep on forgetting her married name even though I have met her husband many times. She has been a fairly regular attendee at Powerstock – sometimes bringing with them some of the cider they make from juice crushed at their cider demonstrations. She is now expecting her second child so they do not get about quite as much as before. The museum is very much worth a visit. It always puzzles me that Dorset has this wonderful collection of old presses and cider making equipment whilst Somerset is limited a couple of small displays on producer's farms and you would struggle to even find that in Devon.

The shop was always a bit damp and Penny was worried about stocking my books as they would curl up! However, I had an email from her early on 2016 saying that the shop has now been refurbished and is stocking a wider range of ciders than before. I will have to get down there soon.

When finding good ciders in Dorset there is still more to find – my goodness I haven't even mentioned Rosie Grant! There will be other Dorset Ciders mentioned in other parts of this book but I don't want to make it too easy – please get out and explore.

The Ring of Bells Compton Martin - Cider and Cheese Festival

On the Sunday before the May Day Bank Holiday Monday the past three years have seen the establishment of the Ring of Bells' Cider and Cheese Festival which to me has nearly all the hallmarks of a 'good cider' event.

It is run in the garden of the Ring of Bells pub in Compton Martin by the owners Luca and her husband Miles. They are London based and mainly visit the pub at weekends with a manager running it during the week but they certainly seem very involved with it and determined to make the pub very much part of the local community.

It is a smashing pub with a number of rooms and although very recently refurbished with polished wooden tables for the extensive food trade it already feels comfortable and has a range of good beers and a bit of cider as well. It is in Compton Martin in the wealthy Chew Valley, just across from the reservoirs and over the hills from the southern sprawl of Bristol making it a very wealthy and desirable commuter distance out.

At the first festival in 2013 I was promoting my book 'In Search of Cider' and was invited as a guest speaker. This was not the easiest task. I had been allocated a room indoors to talk but it was very obvious from the start that on a beautiful sunny day everyone was very happily sat outside, mainly seated on the grass in front of the marquee and that apart from to replenish their cider glasses or get a burger they were unlikely to move. I ended up with a small speaker system and a microphone by the open front to the cider marquee. It was also evident that this crowd was not really interested in the history of cider. I know it is extremely hard to believe but I have to accept that sometimes the public are more interested in drinking than understanding. I adapted my talk to giving a guide one by one to the dozen or so cider makers to be found inside the marquee – all of whom I knew of course from my general knowledge topped up from my research for the book. It seemed to go down pretty well – though the book sales were rather limited!

The following year I took on a stand for myself – Stone's Bittersweet Cider. Unfortunately Richie was otherwise occupied so I had to do it myself. It was the first time we had tried anything like this so it was very much an experiment. I think we did alright, I certainly sold as much cider as expected and more than covered my costs – though competing with 15 other producers was a challenge.. Luca had organised a competition so that punters had to fill forms to choose their favourite cider and that cider then became the cider that the pub would stock for the year. The competition encourages some members of the public to go around every stand getting small tastes of cider with absolutely no intention of buying any, though for every one of these there are plenty who are buying!

I know that following this second year a number of the cider producers had decided that it was not a commercial enterprise for them and had not returned. However their place had been taken by a host of fresh producers – some of whom may not have been all they seemed.

Still there were a lot of friends there. It is a chance to catch up with Keith Balch of Piglets Choice who is probably the most local cider maker to Compton Martin being just the other side of the Blagdon reservoir at the wonderfully named Nempnett Thrubwell. Keith has access to one of the few specimen orchards of Perry pears in Somerset and it is always wonderful tasting the different perries he has. Ben Crossman is there from Congresbury where, as the closest producer to Weston-super-mare and Bristol, he picks up a good market for his farm house ciders with apples from his excellent cider orchards. Another local is Darren Wilcox and his family from Shipham near Cheddar. He makes some very good traditional ciders. Rich's cider from near Highbridge were there in the persons of son George, his girlfriend and his young sister Molly who is now quite a tall teenager.

Bennet's cider from Edithmead, Highbridge was also there with their battered old horse box which for some reason they stick to. Viv Bennet, a wonderful old rural farmer who it repays time to engage in conversation but he does not come out to many events. You are more likely to be his wife along with one of the sons. It is very traditional cider for the real purist who is used to having their mouth puckered – possibly safer drunk with a lemonade top. Hugh Trip of East Pennard was there with his fruit wines – fortunately he did not bring any of his even more 'traditional' cider. He liked me suffered from ending up in a tucked away round the back plot. Honey's cider from near Bath was there. They make a good clean light cider and are a favourite of mine. Newcomers included Millwhite from Rooksbridge who seem to have a focus on ciders that have been matured in spirit barrels. The rum taste is not my favourite but it is good cider. They have gone down the route of small 330ml bottles, about half a pint. This seems to be a growing fashion and for them probably a sensible one. They are a business with two bases split between Somerset and St Albans and their sales have a definite London and restaurant bias.

As well as the cider tent there is also a cheese tent in which some of the still strong array of local cheese makers sell their wares. Cider and cheese go together well and it was good to see old friends like Keen's Cheddar from near Wincanton who are one of only three producers of traditional unpasteurised cheddar. This is certainly strong tasting cheese. The Goulds from just down the road from me in East Pennard were also there as were the Bartlett Brothers from North Wooton with their organic sheep and cow cheeses. Another visitor is Michael Eavis who was there with some of his extended family. They produce a 'Worthy Farm Cheddar'. It is actually made for them by a neighbouring cheese maker of repute. Still it is really nice to see him and his family out socially in very relaxed surroundings.

There is a bit of music, bouncy castles etc. for the children and it is a good occasion for all. 2015 was unfortunately rather blighted by some very heavy catchy showers but we still enjoyed ourselves. One of the highlights for me is the setting up from about 10 o'clock in the morning. It is always fun meeting other cider producers and there is a genuine friendly feeling between them though they are ostensibly in competition. There is a discussion what price is going to be charged on the day. Stands are largely allocated on a first come first served basis and I must admit I rather mucked it up. People come in to the marquee with the stands around the edge and tend to circulate one direction or the other. The middle of the back of the marquee seemed to be a good idea. However the late arriving stands were put in the middle of the marquee in an extra row in front of me which rather blocked off the circulation and the action seemed to mainly take part in the front half and the sides. I along with one or two others did not have the traffic that others did

I was delighted to see the excellent Hecks cider from Street back. They are excellent cider makers with some great ciders including their wonderful single varieties like Kingston Black, though sometimes I feel they rather over sweeten this.

As I have mentioned many times, just about all ciders naturally ferment out fully dry. Sweetness, apart from in specialist keeved ciders, is added back in, either with sugar and then pasteurised or with artificial sweeteners. Most cider experts will suggest that the best ciders tend to be the dry ciders. But there has been 'public pressure' or 'meeting what the market demands' to provide over sweet ciders, despite the governments concerns over the amount of hidden sugar in our diets. However some of the ciders that were on offer from many of the producers here, to my mind went too far. Somewhere definitely in the category of alcopop rather than cider.

I will excuse Sandford Orchards from this. They had come up all the way from Crediton with their personable salesman Dan running a very commercial type bar with their keg cider, the medium sweet Devon Mist. They also make some very good other ciders. Orchard Pig were there, with another keg bar set up. Nice people, but their chilli and lime 'cider' is extremely sweet. Orchard Pig still try to maintain the impression that they are a small artisan producer from West Bradley as they were when I first knew them, with images of Old Spot pigs in their orchard. In fact they have moved a long way from this and their ciders are currently produced in Shepton Cider Mill and they have invested heavily in modern branding.

It is probably just as well that I can't remember the name of a cider producer from somewhere to the west of London who came down with a range of bottled fruit ciders. They were only in about their second year of production and claimed their ciders were going down extremely well as they did on this afternoon. Although there may have been a fermented apple base somewhere these were certainly not ciders as I would understand them. They were all flavoured with fruit syrups of various flavours. I did just try to check that as a small producer they did understand that anything with a syrup in it was a 'made wine' and therefor liable for wine duty. They did not seem to understand what I was talking about.

One of the effects of tasting sweet ciders is that it spoils the palette for any subsequent dry cider. As my stall was further round the circuit people's mouths had been conditioned to sweet and sugar and a few of the people tasting puckered up their mouths. Ciders should always be tasted with the dry first and then move on to the sweet.

Despite my stand position my sales were very reasonable. Fortunately there were people looking for 'good' cider and I sold quite a few pints to the bigger drinkers

– a few of whom were keen to tell me when they came back for their third pint that mine was their favourite cider there!

Does this all matter. 'If the public want to taste sickly sweet ciders surely we should be selling it to them.' 'As small artisan cider producers we can't affect public taste.'

I am afraid I do not fully agree with these sentiments. Yes, artisan cider makers have to make a living but West Country Cider is a traditional product. With better standards of production and more attention to things like spoilage by air, modern artisan producers have raised the standard over the past decade. It is a traditional product to be appreciated and to be proud of. We all want it to be a product that will gain wider appeal with a discerning public and to have a sustainable presence in the vagaries of a fashion driven drinks market. To me pandering to sugar addiction and aping the industrial alchopop products does not seem to be the best way forward. Artisan cider producers have to recognise that they have a responsibility to be educating the public about what 'good cider' is. It has happened in the wine market where fine dry wines are now the norm, why should we not achieve it with cider.

Another aspect that comes through when selling to the public at an event like this is that a good number of the people will only drink cider fizzed up with carbon-dioxide. Those producers selling keg ciders or sparkling bottles certainly did better than the traditional flat ciders. A shame but that is our market place.

But that said the Ring of Bells cider and cheese festival is a definite must when 'finding good cider.'

Devon County Show

The second half of May sees the first of three major county shows held on successive weeks. Devon County, the Bath and West and the Royal Cornwall. All of these have a good part to play in my 'finding good cider' explorations for the year.

The Devon County is the one that I spent least time at – mainly because Old Mill do not have a stand there. It would be excellent on the first day but experience has suggested that although it is rebuilding its farming heritage there are fewer farmers on the Friday and especially the Saturday. However, Old Mill always put in some sponsorship to the show and take a table at the Country Landowners Breakfast on the first day. There is an Addington Fund Reception to go to at the lunchtime so I find myself spending most of the day there.

The Devon Country show runs a good cider competition largely focused on Devon Ciders. Saying that, in the past it has tended to be won by Somerset producers on frequent occasions over the years – and in particular by Nigel Stewart of Bridge Farm Ciders from East Chinnock on the road between Yeovil and Crewkerne. Nigel makes excellent ciders and is one of my favourites. You see his stand on many shows and you know it is always going to be good. He is one of about five cider producers who have a stand in the excellent Food Hall at the show. The competition is also on display in this marquee and as they do the judging the evening before the show opens you can see the results straight away. In 2015 Nigel had not won. The places were nearly all won by local Devon producers – some of whom I had not even heard of. This was put down to the fact that they had ensured they used judges from Devon rather than Somerset. I am not sure I fully believe there is such a direct correlation between the choice of judges and the county they come from but it does tend to reinforce a theme that comes out repeatedly that there are regional variations in cider – and we do tend to prefer that we have been drinking since our youth.

After tasting a glass of Nigel's ciders I explore the other stands in the food tent – they really represent the cream of Devon Ciders.

Gray's Cider have a stand. They are reputedly the oldest cider maker nationally though as with these titles others may dispute it. They are situated on a farm in the hills near Tedburn St Mary to the west of Exeter. They have been making cider there since the 1660s. They make their cider in a purpose built cider house / factory which dates from 1850 and have a considerable amount of local orchards. The current generation farmer / cider maker is Ben Gray who is on the stand with other members of his family and friends at the show. The cider factory is one of traditional design where the apples enter at one level and gravity is used to take you through the process to the barrels for storage which are on a lower level. They make a traditional Devon cider which as with many other traditional cider makers who store in old wooden barrels can sometimes exhibit some negative influences from the ingress of air into contact with the cider. It is a cider farm well worth visiting – and last time I was there they were selling the cider at an extremely attractive price.

Another producer in the food tent is **Green Valley Cider** who are based at the award winning Darts Farm, a massive and very good farm shop only about four miles from the showground. Green Valley was founded and grew from the demise of Whiteways Cider in the 1990s. Whiteways had been the largest producer in Devon by a long way before being bought by Allied Breweries / Showerings and over the years production was steadily moved across to Shepton Mallet. Dr Chris Coles and Nick Pring were senior members of staff at the Whimple home of Whiteways and they set up Green Valley Cider at the then fledgling Darts Farm Shop.

They produce a considerable range of bottled and draught ciders and have been amongst the first of the smaller producers to move into the keg and fruit cider market. The shop they have developed within Darts Farm is now of national renown and has a very wide selection of bottled cider and beers. It is unusual for a cider producers shop to stock quite such a wide range. Well worth a visit for anyone in the area or on their way down the M5 to South Devon or to stock up for a stay in Cornwall.

Chris and Nick are also very involved in 'finding good cider.' They organise with CAMRA the Contented Cow Marquee at the Devon County which brings together most of the Devon Ciders with some excellent real ales.

Sandford Orchards Cider have another stand in the food hall run by the energetic Barny Butterworth. When I first met Barny about seven years ago, he was basically a farmhouse maker just going through the duty limit. Of all the young makers he has had the biggest growth and has a wide innovative range of ciders, bottled, draught and Keg. He even has his Devon Mist cider on keg in one of the local pubs in Mid Somerset which also stocks my cider. He invited me to go and see his recently purchased old cider factory in Crediton which I will certainly do later on in this book so I will write more about him then.

Tim Beer who runs **Marshwood Vale Cider** from Dorset had an out of county stand here. An interesting geographical hybrid. He is now based right on the corner of Dorset, Somerset and Devon with most of his cider actually being made by himself on borrowed kit in Somerset but with the apples coming from all three counties. When I first met him he was actually crushing at a cider shed in a timber yard in Devon. Over the past six years he has widened the range and quality of his ciders but they are still very much rooted in natural traditional West Country cider mode. Tim is a great character who is always willing to give an opinion on everything and everyone in the cider world!

Ashridge Cider from Jason Mitchel also has a stand and is one of my very favourites. He started making premium top of the market bottle conditioned ciders over 20 years ago. This is still the core of his business but he has now expanded with 500ml bottles, draught and keg ciders. He produces some of the best bottled cider I know. In particular I am a fan of Devon Blush. This is a strong good bittersweet/bittersharp blend cider with just a hint of blackcurrant. Unlike many fruit ciders that you find the taste of the excellent base cider comes through very strongly. For anyone who scorns the very idea of fruit cider this is the product I suggest they try.

Having exhausted the stands in the Food Hall I make my way the short distance to the Contended Cow Beer and Cider Marquee. This is a very long bar with two rows of beer casks all the way along with some excellent beers from Devon. There is an excellent selection of small breweries in the county each with a range of beers. Above the beer casks is a row of bag-in-box ciders, all from Devon and representing most of the county's cider makers. Those who are not also in the food hall include:

Berry Farm from Clyst St Lawrence have a cider or two. The farm is owned by a wealthy Dentist who believes in making traditional organic cider. The apples come from old cider orchards which used to supply Whiteways. David Rowe is the young cider maker and his ginger beard is showing huge promise. They make excellent cider which brings out the strong fruity flavour. Talking to David early in 2016 I understand that although Berry Farm will continue, from the autumn he will leave and focus on his own **Crafty Cider** brand which he has been developing in his spare time over the past few years.

Brimblecome Cider from Ron Barter is present. Ron is a really nice guy who makes a very traditional cider in some really historic farm buildings at Dunsford on the way from Exeter up to Dartmoor. These building are really worth a visit – dating from the 14th century with an absolutely massive screw press. In the past couple of years Ron has been rather distracted trying to make a financial success of running a nearby pub. He is one of those producers who stores his cider in old oak barrels. Sometimes he tends to store it a bit too long – I have had cider that was made 11 years previously. I am not sure that this improves the cider!

There were two cider makers in the tent who I had not heard of before. I checked out the website of **Branscombe Vale.** It seems to be a part of the excellent Branscombe (Branoc) brewery who make some good beers. However the web site says that the cider is made for them by the **Lyme Bay Ciders.** Lyme Bay mainly make a wide range of fruit wines and liqueurs. They are connected with the Annings range of fruit ciders. They have told me that their cider is actually made from juice provided by Julian Temperly in Somerset. Their range included the deservedly popular Jack Ratt cider brand named after a local smuggler.

The other Devon cider I had not heard of was **Crebers Rock** from South Brent. Their web site give little clue about then other than they are making organic cider on a small scale from local apples.

Most of the other producers I was more familiar with. **Countryman Ciders** is run by Vernon Shuttler who is the long serving treasurer of SWECA the South West Cider Makers Association. It is quite a trek to his cider farm in the extreme South West of the county. The address suggests it is near Tavistock but in fact you have to drive into Cornwall and out from Launceston to get on the right road. It is one of those places that you are amazed anyone finds but a lot of his trade comes from tourists in his attractively set out shop. Good clean cider made with a selection of Devon and Cornish Apples.

Hunts Cider can be found in the hills behind Paignton. A pocket of orchards which originally date back to the 18th century or beyond. There was a distantly related Hunt's cider which dates from the early 19th Century but this sold out to

Whiteway's in the 1930s. The current connected Hunt family, Richard and his father are of more farm cider origin. When I first visited they were producing in a listed building which was clearly a cider 'factory' dating from 1807. They have had to move out from this building now and have built a new premises and shop. Well worth hunting out.

Palmerhayes Cider just outside Tiverton heading west is run by Aubrey Greenslade and other members of his family. They are well into their 70s and produce traditional 'scrumpy' style cider for the tourist trade in North Devon. Some of this also becomes Cider Vinegar. On a visit there he asked me if I knew anyone who wanted 10,000 litres of cider vinegar he had in a tank!

Reddaways cider comes from a remote farm down a narrow road near Luton – the one near Chudleigh not the one with a football team. It is a farm operation run by the son where the father farms some wonderful South Devon Beef cattle. As well as draught they also make some good 500ml bottled ciders.

Last but not least in this roundup of the ciders in the Contented Cow is **Venton's Devon Cyders**. After early success at the Devon County show Mark Venton has been developing his business with some excellent traditional ciders. He is now almost at a scale where it can support him – as long as he can sell all he has made. Much of his cider is pressed through straw – though as this is a rather slow method with one 'cheese' a week restricting his output, he now has a rack and cloth hydraulic press as well. You can see Mark on many shows and his ciders get widespread around the country on the cider festivals.

One last cider maker I came across at the 2015 Devon County show was **Woody's Ciders** from Newton Poppleford. Woody is the local shop keeper in Newton Poppleford. He has equipped a bright yellow bus as a food outlet and cider bar. The bus was mainly Thatchers cider but he also has his own range of bottled ciders. Buying in juice from Somerset he makes a wide range of fruit ciders from the expected to the bizarre. Fortunately the background cider is quite good otherwise I am not at all sure what I would make of Vimto cider! I think I bought a selection of about 8 different flavours.

The Devon County is a good shop window for most of the Devon Ciders. This is not a complete list of ciders in the county. Others like **Sam's Winkleigh** cider appear elsewhere in this book. There are other delights to hunt out such as

Indicknowle cider near Ilfracombe or Tim Chichester's **Suicider** or **West Lake Cider** miles from anywhere! Devon is one of the main cider counties and exploring and finding different ciders is part of the fun of 'finding good cider'.

Fruit Ciders

I am not such a cider purist that I dismiss all fruit ciders as undesirable. In fact one of my very favourite ciders is a fruit cider – Devon Blush from Ashridge Cider made by Jason Mitchell. It is a really good quality, well balanced bittersweet cider with a hint of blackcurrant. I have judged it as a winning cider in the Taste of the West Awards and I bought a couple of bottles in a farm shop last month.

However, there are far too many fizzy fruit drinks that do not deserve to use the label cider and are basically over-sweet alcopops pandering to a particularly transient youth market. Why is there this variation and how has it come to develop?

There are two historical routes to fruit ciders. Modern fruit ciders are fundamentally ciders with added fruit flavours – often added in the form of a sugar based cordial. For the sake of convenience for this argument we will allow 'Pear cider' to be considered as perry rather than a fruit cider though there are some debatable issues around that. Interestingly many of the 'fruit ciders' made by the larger companies are in fact 'fruit perries' – they use fermented pear juice as the base. There are good reasons for this. I can remember Matthew Showering of Brothers Drinks in Shepton Mallet telling me about it and I have since had it confirmed by some leading large scale cider makers. A perry base take added flavours better than ciders do. In particular with traditional bittersweet ciders added fruit flavours can be distorted and the clean taste effect can be lost.

The first route is the traditional one. If you go back to the 17th century historic books on cider production such as Worledge and Evelyn it is quite apparent that a wide range of fruits and spices were being added to ciders – particularly the hedgerow fruits. In fact these books are really fascinating to show the wide range of things that people were trying to make alcoholic drinks out of back then. Even down to the sap of trees. There are many types of drinks detailed that we do not see today. As a hobby we have tried to recreate some of them for our own consumption and for Richie to use to accompany some of the lectures he gives on the Golden Age of cider. This was the period when there were the first attempts at creating 'keeved' ciders and the British inventions of the bottles capable of holding pressure now known as champagne bottles.

The cider purists who do not like the idea of a historical basis for fruit ciders claim that they were just trying adding things to make bad ciders, taste better. No doubt there was an element of this – no one likes pouring away a barrel of cider so blending, additives and especially sweetening are perennial ways of making it drinkable. However, this is not by any means the complete answer. They were deliberately harvesting and adding different fruits and flavours to experiment with new tastes – some of these date back to the dawn of cider and before.

The second historical route to fruit ciders is the adding of flavours at the time of purchase. This was widespread throughout the 20th century. I can remember as a student in Bristol in the mid-1970s where the cider pubs all served Taunton Dry. The cider was so dry that you invariably started the evening with a 'cider top', couple of centimetres of lemonade on the top of a pint to just take the harsh edge off. By the time you got to the second pint your taste buds were well attuned and the cider started to flow a treat! 'Cider top' was in reality a fruit cider. As was the popular 'cider and black' – cider with a slug of blackcurrant cordial on the top. A number of modern fruit ciders are recreations of this.

Mulled cider is another traditional version with added cinnamon and ginger plus raisins and other fruits. Usually this was prepared on the spot and heated together and drunk warm. The libation for many a wassail and is always popular on a cold day. This is often now found bottled premixed and of course is another fruit cider. On a cold day many ciders were heated with the addition of gin or other spirits. It is illegal to pre add spirit to any cider – though a number of producers have tried to find a way around this with whisky or rum cask ciders. Claiming that the flavour of the spirit comes from maturing in a former spirit cask. Suffice to say that HMRC view this with great suspicion, it is difficult to be sure if the flavour is coming out of the wood, or a little bit has been left in or added to the barrel!

There is therefore a very long tradition for drinking flavoured and fruit ciders. Therefore why do the cider purists frown so much on modern day 'fruit ciders?'

In the 1990s there was a craze for 'alcopops'. Alcoholic fruit flavoured drinks such as Hooch. For a few years these swept all before them with teenage drinkers and in the clubs. Young drinkers could get absolutely wrecked drinking drinks that tasted like soft drinks and had none of the inhibiting factors that the taste of beer, cider or wine can have. Teenage consumption of vodka especially when mixed with coke fits a similar bill and I can remember embarrassing myself on this as a youngster. Although few realised it at the time one of the leading bottlers of these alcopops was Brothers Drinks in Shepton Mallet who over the past decade have become one of the driving forces in the fruit cider market.

Although they are still made and available - drinks like WKD being particularly popular – the fad for alcopops passed relatively quickly. There was a void in the market place to be filled. The popularity of the cider over ice Magners campaigns quickly led to flavours being added to cider (or perry) and this became the fashionable drink – mainly of the young. Since then there has been the rise of a whole range of flavours. Strawberry Cider was the early front runner but this has been surpassed by things like elderflower and lime, rhubarb and custard and the truly ridiculous toffee apple. All making fizzy drinks that are easy to drink.

It pays to look a bit closer at what there drinks actually are. They are not ciders according to the government duty regulations. They are 'made wine'. The duty regulations do not allow the addition to cider of any fruit or flavour other than apples and pears. This allows ciders and perries to have a lower level of duty payable. The duty on wine and made wine is much much higher. This level of duty means that it is economically unrealistic to make a fruit cider at above 4% alcohol whereas most commercial ciders are well above this. For a start this means that fruit ciders are likely to have about 50% water added to the base. The base may be based on pear concentrate or a low tannin apple concentrate. 'Traditional' cider flavours tend to get in the way of the alcohol free taste that the producers are trying to give young people.

The added fruit flavour usually comes from a concentrated, unfermented fruit cordial. These are usually made by adding copious quantities of sugar to the fruit as a preservative. The whole lot will then have a lot more flavour enhancers, sweeteners and more sugar or glucose added before being pasteurised. The result is all too often a product that has a synthetic flavour and horrendously high levels of sugar.

The big question is should these even be called ciders. Ciders are supposed by law to contain 35% fruit at a specific gravity of 1.330 In many cases it would be worth asking if this is the case – with 50% water to get the strength down they have little to play with.

Further the industry says a fruit cider should be 'cider with…' It is not fermented fruit. The taste should be recognisable as cider. Again this is highly questionable! Though I don't think it would be worth the bill for anyone to challenge this in court.

It is a market which most cider makers – including most artisan producers have taken to. To make their living they need to satisfy public demand and cannot afford to miss out on this sector of the market. Together with pandering to the public taste for sweetness I would very much agree with the purists who claim that doing this is destroying the market for traditional West Country cider. Most of our cider makers have an element of turkey's voting for Christmas!

There is an interesting split in the marketing of fruit ciders which leading manufacturers are keen to develop. There is the very strong marketing to youth, young drinkers with popular fun brands that appeal. These tend to be the strongest fruit flavours like the strawberry or other berry. Then there are a number of companies trying to market more sophisticated flavours to appeal to women and a slightly more mature market. Chilli and Lime, Cucumber and Mint etc. What they all have in common is their sugar laden sickly sweetness – bring on the sugar tax.

There is debate as to whether this market is now growing or not? The figures show that since reaching its peak in about 2009 that cider market is probably down at least 5%. I am not party to all the statistics. I have talked to important figures in the industry who think the future is for new and exciting tastes. Their latest justification is a belief that this is what the craft cider market in America will drive it to. I am not yet sure if the American market is all it is cracked up to be. And with the leading brand, Angry Orchard owned by the Boston Beer company and the next two brands actually owned by C&C Brands of Magners fame the depiction of it as a craft driven market can very much be called into question!

There is also a question about how much the fruit cider market is growing in the UK. I have had suggestions from some authorities that it is in fact shrinking at a faster rate than the traditional ciders markets.

I seem to have started on a positive around fruit ciders with Devon Blush and the history and then got into a bit of a rant about the current market. I will finish with describing what Richie and I do with fruit ciders. We do not make fruit ciders to sell – we do not want to get involved with made wine duty. It is just for the consumption of ourselves and the occasional friend.

We make hedgerow ciders with fruit we gather ourselves. Usually blackberry which we have not been over successful with, it tends to have a very dry taste. Sloes – sometimes on their own or sometimes as the residue from making sloe gin. These are usually very nice. Our favourite is elderberry. We gather the berries in September and put in our freezer. In late October we defrost them and mix the berries into our milled bittersweet apples prior to pressing. It is amazing how adding only 3% – 5% gives the juice that runs out a purplish hue and the flavour of the fermented cider is excellent. One year we did nearly 10% elderberry and this can a far too strong a taste. We only make about 40 litres a year – and it is certainly one of my favourite of the ciders we make.

I really don't think that the cider purists can raise any objections to this. I recently found out that this is the only way of being allowed to make fruit ciders in Australia. There currently nothing is allowed to be added post fermentation so all fruit flavours have to be in the pressed fruit.

I am all for innovation in the cider market and believe there is a place for developing different tastes – however the sugar fuelled content of much of the current crop of commercial fruit ciders is something I view with an element of abhorrence.

The Royal Bath and West Show

Late May and the beginning of June sees the Royal Bath and West Show. It is the only remaining regional four day agricultural show left in Britain and is visited by around 150,000 people every year. Some may say it is a dinosaur from a time past. They focus criticism on a supposed reduction of the farming content of the show and say it has just become a commercial sprawl of cheapjack traders. This is such a misinformed statement that it is a wonder that these people are given any credence at all – they have totally missed the point. Of course the show has moved with the times and adapted to modern requirements of a consumer orientated public but it is very much still a country show with the same very strong 'farm meets town' root that is has shown since its inception.

Nearly all the farming shows started in the mid 19th century. The Bath and West Society was founded in 1777 but it was not until 1851 that the first show was held. In fact due to shows missed because of wars and foot and mouth it was not until 2014 that the 150th show was celebrated. One of the main thrusts of these shows was agricultural improvement and the display and sale of new farm machinery as it was invented and introduced. The show had a key role in the improvement of productivity in agriculture from the start right up to current time. However, it is fair to say that with increased mobility and a farming population reducing in relation to the whole that over the past 30 or 40 years innovation in farm machinery has been more focused at more specialist farming shows. Indeed the Royal Bath and West stage a number of these themselves and the first Wednesday in October The Dairy Show is one of the most successful in the country. However, this does not mean that farming is not present at the show, or that farmers do not attend, I know I meet them there and provide hospitality in the Old Mill marquee.

The second thrust of the shows from when they started was the exhibiting of livestock and encouraging the improvement in breeding. This is very much alive and well. The numbers of Sheep, pigs, goats and cattle would seem to have hardly ever been higher. Of course restriction on cattle movement and welfare concerns have made this hard. And with the tight economic times and reduction in the number of people who work on farms it needs to be dedicated breeders who are willing to attend with their stock for four days and pay for people back home to continue with the farm work. However attend they do and with their numbers swelled by huge numbers of smallholders, people who see an element of back to the land as an essential and wholesome part of their lifestyle.

Another feature of the early shows was equestrian. Originally farmers showed off their horses and their skills on them. This grew into the huge range of equestrian events and sports we know today. From show jumping to pony club games there are an immense number of horses and people taking part. The equestrian element really now represents a show within a show.

From the start of these shows the objectives clearly included supporting local business and commerce and nearly every show had well supported art exhibitions, floral displays and competitions. Reading through old newspaper reports it is also very obvious that from the start that they were very keen on increasing the number of members of the public who attended and entertainment was essential, from bands playing to the military displaying.

For the Bath and West two farming sector interests came to the fore in the late 19th century in harness with the desire to improve farming in general. In the pasture heavy West Country the dairy industry was of prime interest. Production of milk, butter and especially of cheese was at the core. Although there are a couple of large specialist shows elsewhere – particularly at Nantwich and Frome, the cheese show within the Bath and West retains its importance, especially with Cheddar cheese which, after all, is a very local product. Now badged as 'the British Cheese awards' there are more entries than ever – though friends of the show feel that the actual presentation of the cheese competition at the show does need to be enhanced. The introduction of a 'cheese village in 2015 was a positive step – but it left the competition hall rather bereft.

And of course the other major farm product for which the West Country is famed is of course cider. During the decline in farmhouse cider from the 1960s until the 1990s this had dwindled to be almost a foot note at the show. Then in 2001 a group of enthusiasts started The Cider Marquee in the cider and perry orchard which had been planted out by local producers Showerings when the show moved to it permanent site in the 1960s. The cider marquee has grown to be one of the major features of the show and in it is held what has become one of the world's biggest cider competitions with over 500 entrants each year. For everyone in cider from the 'national' producers at Thatchers and Shepton Cider Mill down to the artisan and craft producers and to the complete amateurs making cider as hobby the Bath and West has become one of the real events to celebrate good cider. Not only the vast array of excellent products available but also celebrating the heritage of cider and the social fellowship of the cider producers and orchard owners.

The vacuum left by the relative reduction in farm machinery has been more than taken up by the growth of interest by the public in what they eat, how it is reared, how it is cooked and how it tastes. In the 1970s my father sold whole grain mustard in the single food hall. Since then the interest in food has grown and grown. All around the showground there are food producers selling their wares. It has developed from food usually bought to take home to become increasingly 'food to go' which is eaten at the time on the showground. In 2016 we will see the introduction of the new 'food village' taking over the whole centre of the show ground as the development of the show sees the evolution onto becoming a gastronomic delight. Cider plays a huge part in this and tens of thousands of people are seen around the showground either walking or sitting in the sun sipping from a glass of West Country cider.

The set up
Although there are over 200 acres of the Bath and West showground for me 90% of the show happens in a small triangle on the north and west side of the main ring. The Old Mill Marquee overlooking the north side of the main ring, the food halls to the west of the main ring with excursions a few yards south down to the Cheese Pavilion and the Members Tent or back north and west to the Cider Marquee. Although the show is only open for four days for me it lasts for at least eight or nine – and that is not taking into account all the committee meetings for planning throughout the year. Three days set up and one day of breakdown would be the minimum.

This year I borrowed a van from the very obliging Neil MacDonald of Orchard Ground Force and that eased the work considerably. The initial reason for the van was to move boards from my store at the Anglo Baverian Brewery to the cider tent where one of my tasks is to help with the interpretation / history display. Over the years I have gathered a considerable display of material for this, and look after material for other people as well. Promoting the heritage and understanding of cider – what it is (or should be) and where it comes from is a key role for the tent. Where else can we have such an opportunity to engage with the public and the potential cider drinkers? It is a popular aspect to the tent and looked at by many visitors. As some of the elders reduce their involvement it seems to have devolved to me to take on responsibility to see that the display is set up in time. Having helped provide display boards and material, three shows ago for the 150th show celebration I discovered on the Wednesday morning as the show opened that nothing had been placed in the special display we were doing – 'Cider a Journey through time'. My wife, and sons spent a hectic hour with me setting out photographs and documents.

However much advance planning there has been it is the heritage display that always seems to be the one that fits in around everybody else. This year again no one was sure where it would go and how much space there was. The big boards I provided ended up mainly being used for other things. Then on Tuesday afternoon we realised there was a length of the back of a screen that had not been used. We stood some smaller boards from Keith Goverd which had been put back into someone's car as surplus and I then had plenty of room! On the Wednesday morning as the show opened I discovered that an area that had been reserved for orcharding organisation ONE had suffered a confusion of dates and they were not going to be there until the Thursday. A set of boards on the history of cider which I had not used made a quick and adequate substitution. This year of course it will be much better organised – hopefully!

On the Sunday amidst other activity Richie and I get our entries ready for the competition. I think we entered seven classes this year. The farmhouse dry and sweet in gallon demijohns – the most visually successful and prominent element of the competition. We could not enter the farmhouse medium as we were judging that. We also entered the 75cl bottled classed for dry medium and sweet, a single variety class and the naturally sweet bottled conditioned (Keeved) class. Contrary to the belief of many, like most producers we find we do not have time to prepare 'specials' for the judges. We basically take the best of what we have that is ready to drink at the time with a little bit of blending to get some sweetness – which we like to do with cider which has a residual sweetness in it – if we have any available. It is actually quite fiddly to ensure that the entries fit within the specific gravity (sugar) requirements for each class.

On the Bank Holiday Monday other volunteers appear and I spent a physical session helping set out the tables and the special racks for standing the entries competition entries on. There must have been four or five volunteers. Bob Chaplin the senior steward for the tent was of course there. Martin Berkeley was already getting the bar set up and a number of other people drift in and out. My prime concern is gathering all the stuff from the Anglo for the Old Mill Marquee and making a start on building that.

Tuesday is a manic day – to put it mildly. I have to go into work in Yeovil first thing as I won't be back in there all week. However I quickly load the car with more display materials and head back to the show, picking up a draw prize hamper from Jon Thorner's on the way – plus a trip home to pick up the cider entries for the competition.

The cider tent is abuzz with both volunteers – there is a large roster of stewards - and people to help with the competitions – and people dropping in their entries for the competition and meeting old friends when they do so. A very big feature of the cider world is how friendly all producers are with each other – from the largest to the smallest. At the Bath and West there is also a very strong link with the cider orchards. Whereas many cider producers are primarily at the show to sell their cider it is a quieter time of year for those who specialise in growing the apples. On the committee you find Neil MacDonald of Orchard Ground Force, Alison Tilley with orchards near Castle Cary, Jonathan Hoskyn with his orchards and pick your own at North Perrott and by no means least the founder figure of the Cider Marquee Rupert Best with orchards at Hinknowle in Dorset. Doyen of the industry John Thatcher sponsors an orchard competition as a prejudged part of the event. All this adds to the 'good cider' atmosphere of the tent. It is a day of old friend greeting old friends and catching up with each other. Unfortunately I cannot spend long in the cider tent today as I have to get the Old Mill tent set up where there is an unending series of jobs to do from making sure the real ale is arriving from the Milk Street Brewery and has an entry pass to the showground and that Mrs B's the main caterer we use has got all the equipment we need and that the freezer van we hire from them for the week is working. Our hospitality bar also includes a 25 litre barrel of Kingston Black cider from Hecks and of course a box of Stones Bittersweet – in the end we eventually get through two and a half boxes of this to the estimated 1600 people who come through the Old Mill Marquee during the four days of the show.

By about 7.00pm I have set up everything that can be done with just some minor finishing off to do in the morning. I come back to Shepton and collect Richie and we come back down for our customary eve of show walk around. It is beautifully quiet and for me is probably the best time I get to see what is around. We fill a glass each of cider and go for a wander. There are still people around – probably over 1,000 people stay on the site. Some are with their livestock, other traders are still setting up their stands. We always fall into conversation with someone and maybe bring the wheelwright Martin Symes and his wife back to the Old Mill Marquee for another glass. By dusk we return home – ready for the first of the four days of the show.

The cider competition

We are back down the show ground by 7.00 am and get on with the fine detail before opening the Old Mill Marquee. There are visitors around from about 8.00 – going to the Country Landowners Breakfast. By 9.00 we are in the cider marquee ready to get on with judging. In recent years there has been a significant increase in the number of judges. Partly due to the growth of the competition and partly a recognition that there is a sensible limit to the number of ciders a judge can drink. It is only about six years since John Perry and I judged the whole 135 entries in the farmhouse classes! As Chief Steward Bob Chaplin invites the judges and it is an honour to be invited. He spreads it around and not everyone gets to judge every year. There are about 30 judges in all and it is a bit of a mix between the genuine experts, journalists, craft makers and the odd celebrity. It is important to have a good mix of experienced judges. We should be judging for the quality of the cider, not necessarily the most commercially appealing – a distinction that I sometime worry if all the judges are experienced enough to understand.

I am now quite an experienced judge and think I am able to give a good objective view and can spot flaws. There are some judges who are far better than me and have a really good palette developed over many years. The cider judges from the major nationals such as John Thatcher, Bob Chaplin and Bob Cork have superb understanding and taste – the Master Cider Tasters. Then there are the likes of David Sheppy and Mark Rogers, who is now in charge of making sure the judging all goes smoothly. These and others really impress me with their ability to distinguish between good and indifferent ciders. We have frequently asked Bob Cork to taste our ciders and he doesn't hold back! In our first year he explained what mouse was. Once we tried to blend in a very small percentage of cider that was on the edge of going acetic – of course he spotted it. We are given some Bramley apples, Bob spotted it with below 10% inclusion of apples in the cider, suggesting the faint taste of infant apple foods.

This year for the first time Richie is judging alongside me at a major competition. I am delighted with this as I feel he is developing a better ability to judge than me – the benefits of starting younger. We are judging alongside Alan Hogan of Hogan's Cider and doing the nearly 50 entries in the farmhouse medium class. I had not met Alan before and find him to be a very pleasant and interesting guy. He lives in Warwickshire though his the cider is made in Worcestershire. He has come at cider without a huge background of heritage and makes cider largely for the bottled market. He is one of the new breed of commercial cider makers using modern techniques but as far as I can see remaining true to the traditions and his ciders are based on Worcester grown cider apples. Yes they may be a bit more dessert apple and fruity flavoured than we traditionally expect, but still represent good cider.

The demijohns are bought across to us in batches of eight at a time and we sample each deciding which the best is in each eight. Sometimes we put through two, sometimes none, then when we have tasted all we come back and judge the ones we have put through against each other before coming up with a final Gold, Silver and Bronze for the class. In this competition there is only one winner – unlike something like the Taste of the West or the Great Taste Awards where multiple Gold, Silver and Bronzes are awarded. A placing at the Bath and West really means something.

When judging the first criteria is the taste – knocking out anything that tastes in any way unpleasant. Then there are certain characteristics that you are looking for. Firstly that it is appropriate to the class – in this case medium cider. If we have any doubt we use a hydrometer to check it is within the 1.008 and 1.015 specific gravity (SG) band which the class demands. Whether through ignorance – or through trying to pull the wool over judge's eyes this is crucial. Most producers have to sweeten their ciders – but if they do this with non-sugar based ciders they will not alter the SG. We have to rule out a number of ciders that may taste medium but show a 1.000 SG. For those judging the dry classes they have to watch for ciders where sweeteners have been used so that the SG remains at 1.000 but the cider is far sweeter tasting than would be appropriate.

For a West Country farmhouse cider you want to be able to feel some tannin in the juice and the cider must have 'length' to the taste. This is my excuse for not spitting out. How can you judge a cider if you spit it out before you swallow where important aspects to the cider are revealed. A cider that is fresh and fruity on the immediate hit to the front of the mouth can have a much more complex flavour by the time you swallow it.

It is important not to over complicate the process however. If you are tasting one cider against another it quickly becomes apparent which is best and by the use of small batches you are unlikely to eliminate anything that is really good. When I judged with John Perry we had hardly got our taste in when we tasted our third bottle – it seemed good and we kept putting it through. It turned out to be a cider from Rose Grant which won the whole Bath and West Competition that year.

This year there was no clear stand out. The standards have been rising and there were very few bad ciders. However, when we got down to the last four or five you begin to see the wood from the trees and one became our winner for the class. All three of us were very comfortable with our Gold, Silver and Bronze. Please note that we are judging absolutely blind. We have no idea whose ciders are whose so there is no chance of favouritism.

We discovered later that we had selected a cider from Denis France – a craft maker from Wiltshire who sources his apples locally from Somerset – indeed many of them between the showground and Glastonbury. He is an extremely interesting chap whose first interest came from helping his mother with homemade wine making. He is meticulous in his attention to detail and choice of apples and was really delighted to win. We must have done a reasonable job of judging as it them went on to win the best farmhouse cider award for the year when put up against the winner of the medium and dry. Another local maker, Neil Worley, recieved the silver in the class.

The results are put up on a board during the afternoon and some not until next morning – there are other classes still being judged. We popped back a few times to see what our ciders had done. We first discovered we had the bronze in the naturally sweet bottle conditioned cider – the keeved champagne cider. Four years before we had had the second in this class and three years ago we had won it. Testament to Richies attention to detail. We hadn't had a placing for the past two years so were delighted to discover that this year we had the third, bronze placing. It is hard work to make and we only do about 100 bottles a year. Because it is different to our bulk ciders we don't really market it but it is very popular with some friends and we enjoy drinking it ourselves.

We then discovered that we had won a Silver (second) in the farmhouse sweet class. This was of great delight to Richie. It was the first time we had received a placing in the gallon demijohn classes at a major competition. It was a blend which included a lot of juice with arrested fermentation so maintaining residue sweetness. For a time we overlooked that fact that we had also got a Very Highly Commended (fourth) in the farmhouse dry! I think we were in a bit of a daze – three placing at the Bath and West was way beyond our dreams. And it was across a range of ciders. Probably a fluke year and we don't expect it to be repeated soon but it does give us great encouragement that we are getting pretty reasonable at this cider making lark!

Around the cider tent and outside

It was time to explore the SWECA bar next to the competition in the marquee. SWECA – South West Association of Cider makers has about 60 members and Martin Berkeley has sourced a box or two from most of the members where it is practical to go on the bar here. Around 60 ciders from about 40 different producers. It is one of the widest selection of good ciders which you could find anywhere in the country. Yes there are festivals which claim to have over 100 – but closer examination reveals that many come from a limited range of makers. I came across one 'festival' where 45 'different' ciders came from three associated makers. And at these festivals you also find that many are not traditional ciders but alcopops made with concentrate and fruit flavourings. At the Bath and West you have individual tasting ciders crafted by artisan producers and some of the best from a few larger makers.

One of my roles on the cider committee which organised the event is try to balance the finances. Until now it has always cost the show £12,000 to stage the cider marquee – we want to get that down to about £5,000 or possibly break even. Although we would like more sponsorship our major source of income is from the profits of the bar. In the past couple of years Martin has been tightening up on the supply side. Most producers only sell one cider. There is a focus on the bag in box draught ciders rather than bottled ciders on which less margin is made and there is a much closer matching of the quantities of cider bought to the likely sales, with some local producers on standby if there is a danger of running short. This has made a huge difference to the finances whist at the same time probably enhancing the quality of the ciders available. In 2015 we added the sale of pints to halves for the cider and this seemed to boost takings quite considerably. I stick to halves so over the four days of the show I can taste a considerable number of the ciders, especially if I purchase a different half for Richie and possibly Christine at the same time and we have a sip from each other's cider.

Also in the tent is the 'People's Choice' cider competition where each day the public for a pound are asked to judge on 6 different ciders and a winner is put forward to the final on the Saturday. Although the popularity does not back me up I am very sceptical about the value of this. On Thursday it was the day of the medium ciders, or so called medium. I tasted mine which I thought was fine. Four of the other ciders were to me far too sweet to honestly be called medium even though they came from reputable makers. The fifth was not only sweet but carbonated! Not even comparing like with like. One of the ideas of this competition is to educate the public into the variety of better ciders. The event is the brain child of the excellent Chairman of the Cider committee, Anthony Gibson, who is a master of PR so I bite my tongue. It shifts a surprising amount of cider and makes a nice profit for the tent.

Another feature in the tent is the Tutored Tastings where three times a day (twice on Saturday) an expert stands up and delivers a talk whilst the public taste four different ciders. These are great fun and though the speakers vary they can be very educational. This year I had had the task of getting the speaker's programme drawn up. It is not a simple as it sounds as you have to find not only people who are likely to be willing but will be at the show and free at the required time. I started with David Sheppy who had organised the speakers the year before and he was so relieved not to have to do it again that he signed up for two talks. Bob Chaplin and myself were fixed for the talks on the Saturday when there tend to be less producers available. I took as my theme local producers. A fair amount of humour along with some education and samples from Worley's Cider, Stones Bittersweet, Martin Berkeley's excellent keeved cider and I think it was Harry's. All very local to the central Somerset area – and I mentioned all the ones we weren't tasting. The knack is to have enough patter to keep going without pausing whilst the helpers pour the next sample. Both Bob Chaplin and Anthony Gibson seemed to be amused by my talk and reckoned I had got a plug in for nearly everybody. One session which unfortunately I did not see for the second year running was from Dan Heath of Cider Box. I hear very good things about his speaking – he does many cider tastings particularly in London where he preaches the Gospel of good cider – I find out more about him later in this book. In 2015 at the instigation of Mark Rodgers two of the tastings on the Friday gave the public a chance to taste some of the winning farmhouse ciders. A brilliant idea – but with logistical difficulties making sure there is a sufficient quantity around to taste. In 2015 the overall winner came from Sherborne Cider – a producer who only a few of us had met and tried. Simon and Victoria Baxter are apple growers who provide many others with cider apples. They have only been making their own cider a few years. They believe in mixing in some selected dessert varieties and produce a very fruity flavoured cider. Being close at hand they managed to bring in a 20 litre box for the tastings

As well as historic displays the tent and the area outside also contains a good number of cider related trade stands. Equipment suppliers Vigo have a big stand on one side facing both the inside and the outside. Many cider makers get a lot of their equipment and supplies from them. I spent many years looking at the wooden presses which make such a good starting point for the home producing amateur. However, by the time I could afford a press I had already moved beyond that in aspiration. Our Spiegel Mill for milling the apples came from them in our second season after failed experiments with a garden shredder, and our current – third – press came from them. This is a Hydro press where the juice is squeezed out by the power of water filling a bladder, pushing the pomace against the wall of a cage which results in a spectacular egress of juice. Round the back of the marquee were two trade stands which nearly got missed – one selling fine wooden presses for the amateur and one a new rival for supplies to Vigo.

There are two manufacturers of larger machinery present. Somerset Fruit Machinery from down the road in Martock manufacture everything from small push along harvesters to monster equipment for large orchards and vineyards. A lot of their machinery goes to France or is bespoke machinery for the likes of Thatchers. Then there is Core Equipment who have a considerable area in the tent with a lot of items I would like – but Richie repeatedly points out that with our limited time available and limited scope for growth we just should not be considering. It is nice to look though.

Perhaps pride of place is the joint stewards' table, information point and bookstall. Ann does a wonderful job of getting together all the current available books on cider and either buys a small supply or more normally gets them on sale or return from the authors. Surprisingly, though thankfully, she allows us to keep the full price the books sold and this has been one of my major sources of book sales over the past five or six years since I first produced my Somerset Cider Handbook. That and its successors still sell and I am genuinely surprised by the number that sold in 2015 when I did not have a new book. The aim is to have this book ready to launch at the show in 2016, I may struggling to get it ready in time!

Other stands include a barrel maker, usually a college offering a cider making course, and ONE the orchard support network. There has been a long term relationship between the show and the Royal Company of Fruiterers and Rupert Best who founded the marquee is their president this year. Julian Temperly of Burrow Hill cider has a stand promoting his wonderful Somerset Cider Brandy which is not only a wonderful product but also adds a whole extra layer to the cider heritage story. Then there is Lynn and her Somerset Cider mugs. She sells a wonderful range of cider mugs from a good variety of craft pottery's around the county. She also now has a thriving trade in second hand mugs which she has managed to source. These are a real part of the heritage and can fetch a considerable amount of money.

If you enter the marquee from its eastern end you come past The Woodlanders. Taking their name from one of the Thomas Hardy novels which features cider and cider making. These three elderly gentlemen dress in typical Victorian farm yokel costumes. They have with them a large old timber and iron screw press and gradually over the course of the show mill the apples and build a traditional cheese on the bed of the press and make a show of gradually pressing the juice. They represent the epiphany of what the public image of cider should be, a traditional rural craft. Sitting in the sun for four days sipping on a ready supply of cider they probably do more to 'good cider' PR than anything else. They are certainly well photographed! They are led by Rob Mullins, a great character now in his 80s and they have been doing this for about 20 years since they were first got together by Julian Temperley as part of the background in a television adaptation of The Woodlanders. They come from the South Wiltshire Agricultural Preservation Society and are seriously interested in the presses. Fellow members Pete Shipp and Roger Warwick have bit of a collection between them. They feature in my book Dorset Cider. Once you are in the marquee most years you will also see Penny Whatmore promoting the Cider Museum at Overmoigne near Dorchester. Well worth a trip to see a collection of around 40 presses originally collected by her father.

To the north of the Marquee is the orchard planted with cider apples and perry pears which has about 20 now mature trees. This green spot in the middle of the show is a tranquil spot for picnicking and drinking cider alike. Some years that great Gloucestershire cider character Albert Wrixon will be there with his historic steam driver press. Other years it may be Terry Chichester and his donkey driven press – which alarms the show organisers from an animal welfare point of view – especially if he has bought his pet raccoons. There is bandstand where a small group of mature musicians play their gentle jazz numbers – providing a background ambience that the show could do more with. There are occasional displays by morris men who seem to be mistakenly swept up in the current idea of rural heritage.

On a sunny day, especially on the Thursday of the show, many cider makers gather and sit around chatting and discussing the results. Some like Denis France celebrating, some as with this year Tim Beer, disappointed. Mark Venton was up with friends from Devon where he makes his excellent traditional cider in wood. It is all very sociable, ad hoc and relaxed. This is what 'good cider' is all about.

The cider stands

All around the showground you may well come across stands selling cider. Some of these are bars run by the big producers like Thatchers and Shepton Cider Mill, but the majority are small stands run by smaller craft and artisan cider makers. Many of these have over the years become a bit of an institution.

I try to get around as many of these stands as possible – but they are so scattered that I can't even claim to be sure I have found them all. On top of this these days there is a considerable presence of Real Ale stands which are worth a visit as well. In this short section I will not give a full listing of the cider stands but mention some of my favourites which have a long association with the show.

It should be remembered that until the start of the cider marquee in 2000 there were only trade stands representing cider apart from a very small competition. This was started in 1982 but was hardly a worthy successor to the cider competitions of the pre-war shows. It was held in the Bees and Honey tent where it had a short section of racking. I used to go and look at the rows of demijohns and think I would like to know a bit more! I also remember that the predecessors of today's Shepton Cider Mill had a stand that promoted themselves to farmers wanting to plant orchards, but even to me as a fan of apple trees this stand was not really catering for public interest.

Sheppy's was the first of the trade stands. Richard Sheppy, father of David who runs the business now was an enthusiast of the show. They were in the food hall which did not expand until the mid1980s with the Somerset Food Hall when interest in local food began to escalate. The Sheppy's stand seems to have altered very little to this day – I think it is even in the same position in the same spot. Compact with the three metre bar facing outwards and stock displayed behind.. They were pioneers amongst smaller cider makers both with their range and their packaging. They sold the traditional dry, medium and sweet but on top of this had a good range of bottled ciders for people to buy and take away. When Christine and I first started going to the show a litre bottle of Bullfinch was invariably a treat we bought ourselves at the end to take home and drink. Drinking at the show at that time was mainly limited to the five bars/ pubs around the site.

Another early stand holder was Hecks Cider from Street. They got a corner position in the adjoining hall. They have a bar with behind it a rack of barrels which they fill during the show. Brothers Andrew and Chris Hecks take it in turns to do days at the show so you are unlikely to see them both at once. Father and mother still help out – though father is now getting frail. Their respective wives and in-laws also help on the stand and now they are also helped by their children. Andrews's daughter Lizzie has won the perry competition in her own name.

Moving forward Nigel Stewart of Bridge Farm was another long term stand holder whose product I got a taste for and enjoyed a chat with. In 2014 he pulled out of the show feeling the combination of rising stand costs and increased competition meant it was a commitment that could not be justified. However he was back in 2015 with a new stand outside the food halls as the only cider producer in the new Cheese village. I understand he did pretty well here which is great news. Another stalwart who has stuck to the food halls is Chucklehead Cider. Mike and Liz come up from Sussex to attend the shows though the cider comes from Mike's father's smallholding on the Somerset Devon border on Exmoor.

The Bath and West do seem to be in danger of spoiling things by letting more and more cider stands in and also, it has to be, said not always checking on the quality of the cider on offer. There have been a number in recent years who I would definitely not have had space for myself.

The number of cider stands – particularly in the food halls is getting too many. I particularly felt sorry for the excellent Neil Worley who found himself in a dark back corridor of the food hall where there was always a crush of people and people were just swept past his stand. It certainly wasn't a commercial success which is a real shame as his cider is excellent.

In 2016 the food halls are going to be swept away and there will be the introduction of the 'food village' on what was the village green. This is based on the idea that people want to eat and drink at the show as well as buy to take home. As well as the stands there will be entertainment and plenty of tables both inside and outside. I hope all old friends from amongst the cider stands will be there and get good plots

I am encouraged by the experience of one of my favourite cider stands of recent years. Rich's Cider from near Highbridge. They have had an outside stand for many years and although on odd occasions the show have forced them for go elsewhere they now seem to be a near fixture opposite the main ring – just along from the Old Mill and NFU Marquees. Jan Scott took over Rich's cider in 1998 when her father the legendary Gordon Scott died. Her two sisters are still involved with the business and cousin Martin is the well-respected cider maker. But it was the ebullient younger sister Jan who moved the business forward. At the show her husband Brian does the longest hours on the stand and is now helped by both son George and even daughter Molly. I have drunk Rich's cider for many years and its most notable feature is that it is light and very sinkable – not all ciders are!

Around the stand they have a number of tables and it has the features of an open air bar which is well populated by 'regulars' and visitors alike. They do a roaring trade in filled 4 or 5 litre containers. Especially from people who are buying them on their way back to the car park. It is amazing how many people take a container of cider away from the show with them. You would think that they can only source good cider at the show. Sadly there is an element of truth in this, for those living in Bristol or Bath they are not likely to find draught cider to take home for sale unless they really go and hunt for it.

The other feature of Rich's cider stand is its relaxed atmosphere. Especially to closing time. The food halls shut at about 5.30 and trade stands are encouraged to finish by 6 o'clock. Why? There is nothing better than unwinding into the early evening – waiting for the queues of traffic to die down. There are still people around the show ground until seven and beyond. Indeed the main ring activities often do not stop until seven or later and there is often still competition going on in the equestrian rings. I sincerely hope that the new food village adopts this relaxed approach to closing time. It is wonderful for the customer experience and if they want to keep people coming back to the show year on year customer experience has to be key.

Cider is very good for the Bath and West Show and the Bath and West is very important for the whole concept of 'good cider!'

Cider in Cornwall

I finish unpacking from the Bath and West on the Monday and by the Wednesday early afternoon I have loaded up again and am on my way to set up at the three day Royal Cornwall Show at Wadebridge.

The Royal Cornwall is a fantastic agricultural show – though very different from the Bath and West. The Cornish farming community really take it to heart and every Cornish tractor dealer or agricultural merchant has a stand there, along with many national agricultural businesses. All the dealerships take on large stands and there is no shortage of people offering hospitality to farmers.

For a number of years now Old Mill have shared a stand with Towergate Insurance. It has a good spot right opposite the entry to the members pavilion and most importantly allowed us a way into the show which very much favours Cornish businesses – we still do not have an office nearer than Exeter. However after a couple of years I plucked up courage to go and see Chris Riddle who has run the show for many years following on from his father. He was more than happy to see us there as we look after a good number of prominent local farmers – and welcomed the opportunity to get some sponsorship from us. The marquee offers hospitality to farmers and the surprising thing is how many of these are the same farmers we saw the week before at the Bath and West! With first cut silage complete and half term out the way many farmers from Somerset, Wiltshire and Dorset take the opportunity to have a few days break in Cornwall and take in the show at the same time.

Excellent though the show is, because of the different agricultural geography of the area it does not have the same focus on the two key products at the Bath and West. The food halls are restricted to Cornish producers and though you can find local cheese – Cornish Blue is very much one of my favourites – and two or three local ciders, there is not as much competition and diversity as at the Bath and West. However, that does not stop me making the best of the ciders that are on offer!

I started looking at cider on the way down. When I wrote 'In Search of Cider' a few years ago I found reference on the web to Haywood Farm Cider. At the time it talked about making a small amount of cider mainly from culinary fruit. I gave them a mention in the book, but did not know any more. When I had come down to Expo Cornwall earlier in the year I noticed that they had new signs directing traffic off the main Atlantic Highway about three miles before Wadebridge, in fact only about four miles from the showground.

My journey had gone well and I had a little bit of time to spare so I decided to investigate. I followed the signs off the main road expecting to soon find Haywood Farm. It was considerably further than I anticipated. When following signs down narrow Cornish lanes it feels like you are going for miles. Fortunately there were regular reminder signs and despite what seemed like doubling back on myself I eventually drove down a farm track an pulled up at a barn which had an obvious shop for cider sales. It is always best if the setup is professional. Having to knock at a farmhouse door having carefully avoided a snarling dog on a chain, or having to wade through 100 yards of cow slurry may be authentic but hardly makes for a great visitor experience. However, here the shop was smart, opening hours (surprisingly long) appeared on a notice and although I did have to wander down to another barn a few yards further on I soon met the man himself.

Tom Bray must be in his early 30s. He made me very welcome and we soon got talking cider – and tasting. He is making about14,000 litres which is still a relatively small amount for an artisan producer but he has his own orchard and has planted more trees which are coming on stream. I asked about the culinary fruit and was delighted to learn that he now has predominantly cider varieties with a good percentage being of traditional Cornish varieties around which there has been a good deal of work over the past decade. He sells most of his cider in 2 or 4 litre containers with a dry medium and sweet with an attractive label. It tasted like a good traditional cider slightly on the fruity lighter side which is very popular at the moment.

According to the leaflet his family have been on the farm since 1919. It is a quite small farm and if I remember rightly for the past 30 years Tom's father had been more into poultry and poultry equipment than farming with much of the land let out. Tom has now bought more of it back in hand and planted orchards whilst creating some ponds. The aim is to encourage people in for tours of the orchards – and maybe a bit of food afterwards.

Another feature that I was really delighted to see is than on Thursday evening he holds a 'Cider Barn' for want of a better description. The press and barrels are in the lower building I referred to and on Thursday nights his friends and fellow cider enthusiasts come around for a session. Some of the barrels are full of cider made by several of the friends and they enjoy a sociable time tasting them. I visited on the Wednesday and I was invited to the session the next night – however after a very long day including early evening receptions at the show I was rather disappointed that I could not fit it in. However in the meantime Tom and his friends had come and visited the Old Mill stand at the show and I had been able to give them some of my cider to taste – they seemed to enjoy it!

It was really nice to meet a new producer who had his roots so firmly in the traditions of cider. Much later in the year on a weekend break to Cornwall I came across his cider in a pub in Boscastle and it was just as good as I remembered. Definitely somewhere to make for on any trips to the north of Cornwall.

A few years ago there were very few cider makers in Cornwall – however I am pleased to say that the number is beginning to grow –they should be quite successful, after all with the huge number of tourists to the county they have a massive potential market on their doorstep – if rather focused into the summer months.

I have already spoken about meeting Barrie Gibson of Fowey Cider and his excellent bottle conditioned cider at the Taste of the West Trade Show in February. I was very impressed with this product – even if I do struggle with the business economics of a product that has to be stored for so long and has to go through a number of processes. A few weeks after the Taste of the West Show I made my first visit of the year to Cornwall to an Old Mill stand at the Expo Cornwall trade stand. Although this has a food and drink focus it also has gifts and other items. It is a show that seems to be attended by hordes of people who run bed and breakfast guest houses – well it is Cornwall! I was amazed to find Barrie had a stand right next door to mine so I was able to chat to him quite a bit more – nice guy.

There were two other cider makers at Expo Cornwall in March both of whom were also at the Royal Cornwall Show. David Berwick of St Ives Cider is a very interesting character. Also in his 30s he comes from a wine making family in Suffolk. I passed their vineyard on a number of occasions when my parents lived in Suffolk for a few years – but not being a great wine drinker I never went in. David is another who got a 'stop press' mention in my In Search of Cider book. I was doing a last sweep of the internet and that must have coincided within weeks of his launch. I have met him a number of times since then both on trade shows and he has become a member of SWECA. He bought winemaking methods to the making of his ciders but his big problem has been not having access to cider fruit. In fact for the first couple of years he was making batches of 20,000 litres of cider solely from concentrate. His resultant ciders have been drinkable – the general public would not complain – but to my West Country taste they are well made but rather bland – very much missing tannins. Don't worry he knows my opinion and has taken note. At this show he had the first of his 'small batch' ciders which he made last winter from some Harry Masters Jersey apples – a true bittersweet apple. He has called it Hells Mouth and to me it was like nectar. I was delighted with it. Unfortunately it was only a smallish batch and he had run out by the time of the Royal Cornwall. Anyway he certainly knows how to make cider and seeing him later in the year I learn that he is making more cider from cider fruit for next year. I got to taste the next batch at the same show early in 2016. Called Kirthenwood it has a nice story behind it. An acquaintance had bought a Cornish property with nine acres of totally overgrown garden. When trying to clear the undergrowth he discovered it was in fact an old orchard in need of major renovation. David has had the apples from the first year and has produced a very nice traditional dry cider which has an excellent flavour.

David is still trying to increase the proportion of ciders he makes from apples rather than concentrate. A farmer has promised to plant 1,000 trees for him and he is looking to buy land. Unfortunately small plots of land come at a huge premium as they are snapped up by horse owners and he has not found anything the right price yet. In the meantime as his cider knowledge has increased he has tweaked his concentrate brands of Smeaton and Clodgy by adding some malic acid. This has certainly improved the 'cider' flavour.

The other Cider maker who was at both Expo Cornwall and the Royal Cornwall is Skinners. They are definitely not primarily a cider maker, they are one of a number of excellent Cornish real ale breweries. Their Betty Stogs bitter has been a favourite of mine for a number of years and at the Royal Cornwall they have an outdoor bar just outside the food tent where I find it very convenient to get occasional sustenance. They brand their cider 'Cornwall Cider Co

Previously they were having an own brand cider made for the by one of the big two Cornish producers but for some reason have decided to make their own cider in the brewery. I assume it is to capitalise on the captive tourist market in Cornwall. There is what I assume is an old wives tale that it doesn't do the cider or beer any good when they are both made on the same premises. It should be remembered though that they are made in very different ways and use different disciplines. At the Royal Cornwall last year I was okay with their first batches of commercial cider. I am not sure whether they were making from concentrate – but it tasted like a typical cider from one of the commercial makers. At least it had cider characteristics and a reasonably fruity apple feel. When I asked them at Expo Cornwall how is went that previous summer they said it had sold out very quickly – mainly as they had to throw out half of it as it was contaminated in some way.

This second year I was interested as they appeared to be about to try making a hopped cider – dry hopped with Citra Hops. Richie and I have tried hopped cider and the one we made with Citra was very interesting. However, if Skinners launched the product I couldn't see it at The Royal Cornwall. What I did see however were a Mango Lime and Ginger Cider and a Rhubarb and Custard Cider. 4% alco pops. My interest abruptly diminished.

The big two producers of Cornish cider are Healy's Farm House Cider and Cornish Orchards. Both have large stands in the food halls at the Royal Cornwall Show. They are very popular and busy stands – selling mainly bottles to take away. So busy it is impossible to talk to anyone and they are manned largely by merchandising staff. However I had a chance to chat with both companies in October when the SWECA AGM was held at Healy's Cider Farm – well down into Cornwall but with the upgraded A30 these days not quite a quick journey from Somerset.

I have a soft spot for Healy's – it has grown massively since I first took my children on the tractor rides around the orchards 25 years ago when we were tourists. It is a very large tourist attraction. They estimate that during the year around 400,000 tourist's visit which is a massive number. It has the advantages of being a dry place to visit when it is raining on the beaches a few miles away – plus it is free entry! It makes its money from its massive farm shop and restaurant which are attractively set up to persuade people to part with their money both on the premises or to take away. The heart is still around an old farm yard where my young sons enjoyed looking at the farm animals before they knew what cider was. There is also a very good museum of cider bygones, a distillery, a cider mill with a large belt press which you can see and which they use to make their 'craft cider products'

When I arrived for the meeting I was greeted by John Healy – the founder and father of the business who I had not met before. When I wrote about them a few years ago I met John James who was manager and I have also met Sam and Joe Healy the two sons who are now driving the business forward. At first I was slightly disorientated as where I thought the modern factory was there was now a totally new building which we toured during our meeting. Incredible. From an airport style atrium you enter a mocked up stainless steel silo and climb a circular staircase to arrive on a balcony overlooking their ultra-modern bottling plant. A fascinating spectacle with lines of bottles running everywhere. Although I suspect the facility could cope with a lot more it is being run with bottles of their main line – Rattler – a cider which was named after an old Cornish apple variety but marketing wise has become inextricably linked with a cartoon representation of a rattlesnake. It is quite a good keg cider – perhaps a bit drier than some and refreshing for that. There is also a pear version and a blackcurrant version.

They also make a craft range of ciders in 70cl wine bottles. I have judged these in competitions and rate them very highly – perhaps a bit sweet but isn't everything. They are quite strong and rather expensive. Especially those bottles where the cider has been matured in the barrels from the distillery. Wonderful tasting products though.

The other big Cornish cider makers is Cornish Orchards and the founder Andy Atkinson was at the meeting – resplendent in a tweed suit and waistcoat. Andy is a very interesting character who I have a lot of time for. He was a former dairy farmer, a tenant farmer of the Duchy Estate. However, the dairy industry went through a considerable shake up – especially with the introduction of milk quota. He became disillusioned and looked around for something else to do. He made some apple juice from the apples which grew on his farm and it grew from there. Much of his farm is now planted out to orchards and he sources other apples from the West Country.

They make a wide range of good ciders which in Somerset you mainly see in bottles in the supermarkets. They are very well made ciders mainly on the lighter side. Probably a little bit light for my taste in cider but definitely quality products. Andy sold the business a couple of years ago to Fuller's, the major London based brewers. It was the first time I had seen him since then and was relieved to find him still very much in charge. I suspect the sale was a way of getting some much needed major investment into the business.

I very much enjoyed the SWECA meeting – it is always great to meet up with about 40 different cider makers – even if for the vast majority of us the bottling line we were looking at was beyond even dreaming about! However, as I had driven down to Cornwall I also took advantage by visiting Haye Farm Cider – down the lanes on the east side of the Fowey estuary. This had provided me with the highlight of my research for my 'In search of Cider' book. I had arrived in the farmyard suspecting the farm had ceased cider production and been sold. It said toot your horn so I did and Alix came walking up the yard with a bucket of apples in her arms. I asked if the farm was still producing and she told me the wonderful news that it had been bought by a chap called Bill Coles who was the only one of the prospective purchasers who had shown any interest in the cider. He had just made Alix and her husband Neil the tenant farmers making them the fourth generation of cider makers on the farm.

It had a very traditional cider making set up with wooden barrels and an old screw press – and the cider I tasted was sublime. I bought some and took some home for Richie to taste – he took one sip and looked at me with amazement. It was a barrel that had somehow been forgotten during the sale – been rediscovered and only recently tapped – a wonderful experience.

I have subsequently met Bill who is a really lively character with plenty of interests in London but he splits the time between there and Cornwall with his young family. He also has an interest in a Cornish restaurant at Lerryn Quay. However this was the first time I had been back to the farm and met Neil as well as Alix. With that build up I was worried I had set myself up to be disappointed. There was a slight problem but I was definitely not disappointed. The farm was a bit of a building site. A lot of the older farm buildings had basically fallen down in winter gales' and had had to be rebuilt. Work on this was nearing completion and I was delighted to see that they had been rebuilt and reroofed in the totally irrational way of old farm buildings, far too low to be of practical use. They had rebuilt around the old mill and press and reroofed over the old oak barrels which were still in position.

They had had a really poor season for apples last year and had only managed to make about four hogsheads. They have now planted out a lot more acres of orchard with old Cornish varieties and reckon they are in for a bumper crop for pressing in 2015. I tasted one some of last years' cider and reassured myself that the wonderful cider I had previously tasted was not just a lucky freak. It wasn't, the wonderful taste was still there. It must come from the mix of apples. However, today's sample came from a half empty hogshead that had been open for a month. It was beginning to turn – just a hint of acetic. Others I have spoken to have spotted this when they visit Haye Farm. It is a feature of air getting in to wooden barrels – sometimes even before they are opened and certainly after they have been opened. Maybe now they have got the building sorted they can have a think about ways to store the cider which will not allow it to deteriorate – I am fully convinced that the starting product is very well worth making the effort with. It is still the best ever farmhouse cider I have tasted!

Much to my surprise I discovered another Cornish cider maker when we went down for a late autumn break weekend. It was unseasonably warm – you would not expect to be sitting out on a pub veranda at Trebarwith Strand watching the sun go down in November. I had made Facebook contact with a Lorraine Turnbull of Spotty Dog Cider and arranged to pop in and meet her. Like Haywood Farm she was just off the main Atlantic Highway and even nearer to Wadebridge. She is a bit of a writer and has been a lecturer in smallholding matters. She is still very inexperienced in cider making terms but has good plans. Her engineer husband has fitted out a small building with an excellent home fabricated hydraulic press. The previous year she made about 3,000 litres and was aiming to exceed that this season with cider taking a bigger part in her life.

As with many people outside the main cider area her problem has been sourcing the right apples. Any number of people offer her cookers and dessert apples but she has appreciated that this does not make the best blend for cider. She has planted out quite a few bittersweet varieties and some of the traditional Cornish Varieties and paid more attention to getting the right blend. We tasted one of her last bottles from the previous season. A well-made cider but probably at least 40% Bramley – just a bit too acidic without the tannin. She is saying all the right things so I look forward tasting her cider again in the future.

And we did meet the Spotty Dog! A gorgeous young cocker spaniel – mainly white with a few small black patches. I think it is a wonderful name for a cider.

Yorkshire - On holiday

Cider is not now restricted to the West Country – it is available anywhere though often the choice away from the West Country is limited to large producer kegs and very little else. On our 2015 holiday in July to the Yorkshire Dales we certainly didn't go out of our way to hunt cider – however our searches for real ale seemed to lead us in to finding some pretty reasonable ciders.

Although I am quite a fan of JD Wetherspoon's pubs the good range of ales and the cheap and effective food, I am not always a fan of their selection of ciders. I always find they have an unimaginative keg cider and if you are lucky in one of their glass fronted fridges they will have a box or two of some of the Weston's cider brands. This is a shame as in terms of stocking real ales they have always had a good ethos. From recent visits I worry this may be changing. Some pretty boring imported American craft beers – or American craft beers brewed under licence in the UK seem to be taking over. These have to be viewed as a major step back for real ale. Similarly their cider seems to have gone down the route of imported American Ciders – ignoring the sad truth that as the Americans don't have cider apples their attempts at cider are poor fizz with thin bland flavours.

However we are sort of in luck. We have gone on holiday in mid-July whist the Wetherspoon pubs are having one of their twice a year cider festival fortnights. We have gone to the Wetherspoon's Ralph Fitz Randel Hotel in Richmond Yorkshire mainly looking for lunch. However, finding the cider festival on our priorities change. Richie and I each get a pint in thirds which means between us we have 12 ciders over our lunchtime two pints. Wetherspoon's produce a nice menu of the ciders on offer which is great even if it also gives rise to alarm and despondency. On the front of their menu the headlines read.

'Featuring rare and unusual flavours including wild raspberries, bourbon and rum, marmalade cider, elderflower and black berry, whisky cask cider.'

It is a cider festival, why do they have to highlight such awful non cider features? As it is made in Shepton Mallet cider mill under the sadly debased Orchard Pig brand we try the Marmalade Cider. What a peculiar blend. I have an open mind but am not sure why anyone thought this was a good idea. As there are about 12 of the 30 ciders listed for the festival available we have plenty of others to try as well. Of the 30 listed in the catalogue 8 would appear to be 'made wines' with added fruit flavouring – around 4% alcohol so plenty of added water - which pay a higher 'made wine' rate of duty. There are also two spirit infused 'Barrel aged' ciders which should be treated with suspicion. If I want to add rum or gin to cider I would rather do it myself as has been popular in pubs as a warmer on cold nights for many years.

There are a number of cider makers I have never heard of before. And I suspect that fulfilling the exacting task of meeting the Wetherspoon's volume demands may have challenged some of them. One cider we tasted definitely had a strong hint of rather rough farmhouse scrumpy about it, the sort of cider that got cider a bad name and which producers have been keen to move away from in recent years. Although they appear under a variety of different names to those in the know there is no disguising the fact that a number of the remaining ciders come out of large scale producers factories rather than the rather cleansed descriptions they are given. However included on the list are Rich's, Hecks, Sandford Orchards, Hunt's and Green Valley so no West Country cider fan dare complain. I found the Hecks product particularly reassuring.

We are staying near the delightful village of Reeth at the end of Swaledale. After South Shropshire this is one of our favourite bits of the country to visit. Really quiet, wild, wonderful birdlife and other nature to admire and a good selection of pubs and beers.

The Buck House in Reeth is a busy pub that does good food – a good choice of real ales and six different 'real cider'. They mean draught cider in bag in boxes. There are some standards from the like of Rosie Pig from Weston's, some from the Shepton Cider Mill under various brands and at least one Gwynt y Ddraig – Welsh cider made by Andrew Gronow who learnt his cider making in Somerset (I worked under his father for a feed company for a number of years) and I believe it is made mainly from apples imported from England. I suspect all these ciders come from one wholesaler who is bravely pioneering ciders up north. It is great that the cider movement is spreading so far. It is just picky of me to suggest that it would be nice to have a proper dry cider – many of these taste on the sweet side of medium.

During out stay we go a couple of times to one of our favourite pubs. The Tan Hill Inn – the highest pub in England. It is a good pub but the very best part of it is the drive there. It is literally miles from anywhere. If you approach it from the east you seem to travel about five miles over desolate moors before suddenly this wonderful pub emerges before your eyes. It must be well over 30 years since Christine and I first went there on an evening drive around and it took me a long time to overcome my surprise that not only was there a pub in this remote spot but that it was also open!

To be fair it does not have a great range of ciders. It has an excellent range of beers and talking to the co-owner he reveals his passion for the beers but says he would love to have more ciders but there is trouble getting the wholesaler to stock them. But there is one surprise – for the last few visits probably dating back about six years there has been a tap with the legend Sheppy's Cider on it. The website currently says it stocks Sheppy's Raspberry Cider. I had discovered before that the other co-owners now own a centre in Somerset near Taunton and they started bringing boxes of Sheppy's cider with them when they came up on business.

On the way back home over the Pennines we made a detour to find the Brewery Tap for the Dent Brewery. Dent is in a small village about seven miles down a valley with a single track almost into Lancashire. The Tap is in one of the two pubs in the village so is easy to find and the beers are awesome. However, the pub left me profoundly disappointed. The words 'Brewery Tap' conjured up a good feeling. Certainly not images of a highly polished pub with smart furniture that you felt uncomfortable sitting down in. There was quite a large restaurant area but we were told quite sternly that that was only open in the evening and was fully booked for that night anyway. Talk about making tourists welcome. We eventually established that they did serve a limited range of pub snacks at lunchtime and we had a choice of two or three very formal looking tables to sit at. The barmaid was rather smartly dressed in uniform and despite efforts to engage her about the merits of the different beers appear to be both lacking in knowledge and uninterested at the same time.

When I asked her about the ciders she was nothing short of clueless! However, they did have two very interesting ciders. One was Orchard's which is made by a chap I have met a few times at the Bath and West and SWECA meetings named appropriately Keith Orchard. He produces his Wye cider in the Wye Valley on the border between Gloucestershire and Monmouth using local apples and pears. And very good it is too. He produces in quite small quantities so it is surprising to find his ciders this far from home.

The other cider, if anything, was even more of a surprise – the maker has been dead for the past 18 months. The legendary Frank Naish made cider just down the road from me in West Pennard, Somerset for around 80 years before he died in late 2013. The mantle has been taken up by Paul Chant who when he is not away on one of his jaunts still produces his very traditional Chants Cider. He helped Frank Naish whist also producing his own for the last years of Frank's life until he died at the age of 88. The label said it was Naish's cider and I tasted a pint and can confirm that it was. A very nice, traditional Somerset dry cider with the flavours of the bittersweet apples coming through. When I got back home I made some enquiries and apparently there was still quite a quantity of his cider left and one of the niche cider wholesalers had bought a lot of it. Presumably he was responsible for both of the ciders present in this pub. Cider in an airtight barrel will easily keep for three years and I have drunk it a lot older than that on occasions.

It just goes to show that 'finding good cider' can be a fascinating hobby where luck and keeping your eyes open can lead to some amazing results. It also goes to show just how widespread some good cider now is.

Bottled Cider

Richie and I would count ourselves as somewhat experts on bottled ciders. There are people who systematically post reviews of every cider they drink to the internet and may have drunk more different ciders than us. However, Richie collects the labels he painstakingly peels off the bottles and sticks in a huge file. In one way this is important as a record of cider marketing over the past seven or eight years in another way it is a very interesting reminder to something over 400 different bottled ciders that we have drunk. And each time we try a new one we always discuss with each other what we think of it. Indeed if we only have one 500ml bottle we religiously divide it between ourselves.

For instance last night we had two 'new' ciders. Both of them in the top rank of bottled ciders. The first was a new sparkling variant of Copse House Ciders – Lanshire cider. Copse House have developed a very distinctive branding with a very fine art key logo. On this bottle this had been put on a silver background which 'shouted' out quality – and there is no doubt that the cider matched up to it – as you would fully expect from the craftsmanship of Bob Chaplin with all his experience.

The second cider again came with a very great pedigree. Sheppy's Vintage Reserve. This has long been a favourite bottled cider of mine – not the least as it is a different cider each year, David Sheppy follows the interpretation of vintage as meaning it is the cider produced in a particular year, and for the Vintage Reserve it is the very best produced each year. This was the 2015 version and tasted a worthy successor to the previous years. I think I must have tasted at least six successive years. It is one of the really complex tasting ciders with great depth that makes it a satisfying drink. Yes – we had two excellent ciders last night.

Bottled ciders have a very particular market. To be honest when 'finding good cider' I tend to focus on the draught ciders and particularly the farmhouse draught. I would go for an excellent dry farmhouse cider over and above any bottle. Why is this?

Some bottled ciders are just straight draught ciders put in a bottle and capped. These tend to taste quite thin and you wonder why the maker has gone to the expense and trouble of bottling. On its own it bottling does nothing to enhance the flavour of the cider and some very good draught ciders turn out to be rather disappointing in bottles. This is often the provenance of the artisan maker who does the bottling himself so he has something to sell in bottles at the farmers markets. These cider makers would be very unwise to bottle a product without either micro-filtering or more normally pasteurising. Done properly, and it is not always, this will eliminate the risk of further fermentation in the bottle and the potential for explosions of glass. People who try to sweeten with sugar are taking a massive risk if they do not pasteurise. I have twice been given bottles by one producer of 'still medium' cider, two years apart. On both occasions opening the bottle has led to an explosion of fizz. Fortunately the bottles have held but this is getting into dangerous territory.

The larger scale producers tend to use micro-filtering – to remove any chance of yeast remaining in the bottle. Many smaller producers rely on pasteurisation to kill off any yeast or bacterial activity. Unfortunately whether micro-filtering or pasteurising there is the very real risk of removing some of the character of the original cider. I think this is one of the reasons that excellent draught ciders sometimes taste very thin in the bottle. One common feature of some pasteurised ciders is a 'cooked / stewed apple' flavour where the temperature has possibly not been controlled as well as it should be.

However, nearly all cider makers who are bottling take the opportunity to alter the cider prior to pasteurisation. The main route is to add sugar. More sugar is added than most people suspect and nearly all bottled ciders are altered from their natural state of fermented out dryness to either medium or sweet. To me this is the biggest disappointment with ciders today as in far more ciders than I would care to mention the background taste is of sugar – even to the extent of tasting somewhat sticky. Whilst a little sweetening can bring out extra complexity and flavours too much masks the great flavour of the cider.

Here you can have a great debate as to whether sugar or artificial sweeteners should be used to make a drink to the public taste. Saccharin has been used as an artificial sweetener for nearly 200 years. It does have a rather tart taste which is easy to spot. Richie and I sometimes use one of the sucralose type sweeteners. Personally I much prefer this to sugar. I can taste added sugar on at least two levels and feel and to me it seriously detracts from the cider. Basically this is because it is usually overdone. A couple of years ago we were on holiday in Wales and made a point of tasting as many Welsh ciders as possible. I would not want to generalise but would suggest that there was too little tannin and far too much sugar. I didn't come across one that made me feel that I had found good cider.

I have a further major concern about adding sugar prior to pasteurisation. An increasing amount of bag in box ciders have the same process carried out prior to in line pasteurisation. If you add sugar to a bag in box fermentation will restart and you have the embarrassment of a bag blowing up like a balloon in the pub. It has happened to me and I have seen it quite frequently with other producers. CO_2 gets between the linings of the plastic bag and there is very little that can be done to rescue it. Cider makers should take a breath and think what is in the longer term interests of cider.

Many makers also use this stage to add some more malic acid at least into the blend prior to bottling. This adds a degree of body, bite and complexity to the ciders. I believe it is this, combined with the excellence of the base product that gives many bottled ciders that excellence of flavour which I look for. Done well good bottled ciders transcend the original draught ciders. Obviously there is again the case of doing it well. You cannot make a silk purse out of a sow's ear. The ironic thing is that many of the people writing the reviews on the web do not seem to understand that this stage exists at all. The cider purists are sometimes a bit naïve, I am sure I have been guilty of this in the past and don't pretend to know everything now but at least I have my eyes open.

Most smaller scale producers do not have the facilities to do bottling on any scale. On a small scale it is hard and time consuming work. The usual solution is to send a 1,000 litre IBC of cider off to a professional bottler to do the work for them. And to receive back a nicely shrink wrapped pallet of 1600 500ml bottles. The mathematicians here will notice a frequent complaint from producers that quite a lot of cider seems to have been 'filtered' out. This is a complaint that I can find historical precedence going right back to the 1930s.

A few years ago the principle bottler in this region was 'Brands' in the Forest of Dean. However I think they were over taken by their own success and producers were left with very long waiting times. Perry's of Dowlish Wake near Ilminster in South Somerset now bottle for many of the makers I know. They are excellent cider producers in their own right – now on the third or fourth generation – and do a very good range of bottled ciders. Their 'Dabinett' is just wonderful and has deservedly won a number of competitions.

One of the best things about the wide range of bottled ciders available is that it enables you to come across ciders where you would not usually come across the draught. There are a couple of good cider makers in the Three Counties which I have only ever found at a trade show in Cheltenham backed up by bottles in pubs and off-licences. Severn Cider from the Forest of Dean is one. I have drunk their bottled ciders and perry in pubs and found it to be excellent definitely one to look out for. Another is Abrahall Cider from Herefordshire who make a number of ciders including the wonderfully named Thundering Molly with its great label. These are significant cider makers who I would have missed if it were not for their bottles.

As someone in dedicated pursuit of bottled ciders I have to mention where they can be bought. Supermarkets now appear to have excellent ranges of bottled ciders. Treat with caution. What appears to be shelves full of different ciders on closer examination may turn out to be a disappointment. Many will be the different brands from the large scale cider makers. That in itself is not necessarily a bad thing. I will have elsewhere mentioned the superb Chaplin and Cork – made in Shepton Cider Mill – but many brands from large scale makers tend to be less appealing.

The supermarkets will also contain a predictable range of the larger scale artisan makers. Cornish Orchards, Sheppys, Hennneys, etc. Each of whom make a range of ciders, many of which are good. However you are unlikely to find the real local small scale producers.

If you visit the cider makers themselves they are only likely to be stocking their own ciders so it takes time to find a good range. However there is now a small but growing number of specialist cider off licences. I am not sure how the business model stands up. They seem to need to charge about £1 a bottle more than the supermarkets and will readily complain that that does not allow enough margin. The problem comes from producers looking for volume who sell to supermarkets too cheaply. They have to look after their own business but it could be considered a short sighted approach eroding the whole price of quality cider..

The daddy of the specialist retailers is the shop run by Chris Cole and Nick Pring of Green Valley Cider which can be found within the excellent Darts Farm Sheop near Exeter. On a recent visit Nick proudly showed me the trophy they had won for the second time in three years from a licenced trade association newspaper for winning the best cider retailer in the country. They stock an amazing range of quality ciders not only from Devon but from across the West Country including the three counties. Chris's daughter lives in Gloucestershire so he uses visits to pick up a different selection of ciders.

The Bristol Cider Shop is another of the specialist shops. Situated on the historic Christmas Steps in Bristol they carry a good range of bottles and have one or two draught ciders on at any one time. The problem is that the centre of Bristol is never the easiest place to park – and the steep hill makes carrying any quantity of cider a real problem! Paul Snowman is a real enthusiast and is coming to do a couple of Tutored Tastings for me at the Bath and West.

Elsewhere in this book I mention Simon Day's Three Counties Cider Shop in Ledbury which carries an excellent range. Over in Narbeth in West Wales I discovered the unique Fire and Ice which not only has a good range of bottled ciders – even from Somerset, but makes some pretty amazing ice creams, sorbets and gelato's. I am aware of other shops dotted around. They are usually good at publicising themselves so I suggest you have a look on the internet and find out what there is in your locality.

Another to highlight is the amazing 'farm shop' Gloucester motorway services. They have a very wide range of ciders. However, I am concerned that despite a clear artisan ethos they seem to be gradually focusing on the varied products from larger producers. On a recent visit I was really impressed with the merchandising effort they had made for Martin Berkeley's Pilton Cider – it was attractively displayed in a number of areas of the large shop!

Finally, in Somerset award winning cider maker Darren Wilcock of Wilcocks Cider has just about to open a cider shop on his farm at Shipham near Cheddar. He has already asked me if I would like to sell some bottles to him. There is the slight problem. Richie and I much prefer supply draught in bag in box. We are not on a scale where we could send 1,000 litres to a professional bottler. Every year I do a few dozen bottles to sell at the odd show but they do not usually lead to a product we are particularly proud of. Our Keeved cider is a different matter but we do not produce enough to make it worth trying to sell to farm shops or local delicatessens – too time consuming. For now we are sticking to bag in box – it is what we like to drink ourselves.

Mid Somerset Show

The Mid Somerset Show was not something I primarily came to through cider – but the cider part of it and my involvement with the cider at the show have grown over the years.

It was probably in about 1990 that I first got involved in the show through Shepton Mallet Round Table and our stewarding of cars parking around the main ring. It grew during the mid-1990s when I ran a local garden centre and had a stand there a few times. It really took off in 2000 when as a local historian involved with the show I was asked to write a history for the 150th anniversary in 2002. This was the first time I had been asked to write a book and although it never became a best seller I was and am quite proud of some aspects. Rather than take a straight chronological approach I picked out certain themes – horses, cattle etc and especially cider and cheese.

I have been interested in agricultural history since school days particularly the latter part of the 19th century when agricultural shows were starting was a particular time when very significant changes were happening. Both for cider and cheese the period between 1890 and 1910 was crucial for the evolution of the products that we now know and the improvement of developing the consistent products we enjoy today. Mid Somerset was an area of the country that was centrally involved in this – both with the development of farmhouse Cheddar and the raising of the standard of cider to something that was drinkable.

2001 was a Foot and Mouth affected year and I put on a small display of heritage in the Members Marquee about the history of the show. In 2002 for the anniversary this was built into quite a significant display of agricultural heritage. It proved extremely popular. In 2003 this became a large heritage marquee in the top field and somehow or other I have managed to fill this every year since. I think the record was a couple of years ago when I think there were 18 different displays from about 12 organisations – this is hard work! Cider and cheese always feature in our collection of old photographs of the show and in the artefacts on display.

In about 2012 the long standing cider competition at the show – probably one of the oldest existing competitions – became a bit of an embarrassment to the cheese tent where is had always been held. The cheese competition had grown and was attracting more sponsorship and it was not thought that Cider added to the tone of their competition which is of national importance. The cheese committee was rather split on this – but I offered the heritage marquee as an alternative location and was delighted when it was accepted. Not all is easy – some of those who liked heritage were rather against the idea of people drinking cider in the tent. But we seem to have settled it down. Starting in 2013 we added a small cider bar to encourage some of the local cider makers to promote their product at the show. Each year we have about five or six local makers who are not found elsewhere on the showground.

This now brings that number of different cider makers whose product if available at the show up to about 14. This is a radical change from a few years ago. Although I can trace back the importance of cider on the show at least to the 1930s in the 1990s the cider representation was down to a very popular stand from Hecks Cider the Street based family cider maker. After 2002 the show became a free entry show funded by sponsorship and traders pitch fees. Gaymers in Shepton Mallet became a principle sponsor on the condition that theirs was the only cider on sale. Some of us on the committee objected most strongly to this – pointing out that farmhouse cider had a long heritage on the show. However for a year or two Hecks were banished. Following pressure from committee members however sense prevailed. Hecks and then a limited number of other cider makers were invited back on the proviso that they were members of the South West Cider Makers Association. It could be suggested that following changes in trade stand secretaries there was too liberal an interpretation put on this and an increasing number of cider makers where allowed in.

The 2015 show included stands from:

Hecks Bros from Street. One of my very favourite cider producing families over the years. Although father and mother are still around it is now mainly run by brothers Andrew and Chris and at shows you will see them with their respective wives and just about grown-up children. They have an excellent range of blended and single variety ciders. The stand out ciders are Kingston Black, Browns and Port Wine of Glastonbury. I don't know whether my taste has changed or whether they have made these slightly sweeter. I now find I go more for their straightforward dry blend or their occasional dry single varieties like Vilbrie. Anyway Hecks are amongst the greats of Somerset cider making and their farm shop is really well worth a visit to. Their stand opposite the main ring is an institution at the Mid Somerset Show.

Worley's. Neil Worley gets a number of mentions in this books. He is one of the younger generation of cider producers at Dean four miles east of Shepton Mallet. His cider has really developed over the years and in the past year he has been developing distinctive brands like Red Hen and Harvest Moon. His ciders are all proper blends and he also has them turned into bottled products. He and his partner Helen work really hard to mix producing and selling cider with bringing up their their children. They attend shows and markets on an incredible number of days during the season – sometimes with two shows on the same day. Neil is the bane of the show organisers as he tends to keep his bar open longer than others. I personally have no objection to this as it is great to be able to get a much needed drink whilst packing up!

Wilcox's. Darren Wilcox from Shipham near Cheddar is a regular attendee with his wife and daughter. Having recently had a baby does not seem to stop the daughter who is also in charge of their bar at the North Somerset Show. After giving up their shop at the bottom of Cheddar Gorge they are now opening a farm shop back on their farm not far off the A38. I am looking forward to seeing it – they make excellent traditional Somerset ciders

Pilton Cider. Martin Berkeley makes his cider in Shepton Mallet after pressing in Hornblotton. He makes an excellent naturally sweet and sparkling keeved cider and the Mid Somerset is one of the few places where you can find him on a show. He has dozens of bottles immersed in ice which gives a wonderful refreshing drink. Although he also experiments with keg and bag in box his focus is clearly on the top end of the market keeved product in champagne style bottles which can be found in many farm shops, delicatessens, and restaurants and serious off licences. Martin also runs the SWECA bar at the Bath and West

Lawrence's Cider. John Lawrence from Corton Denham was a new cider attendee at this year's show. He has converted a horse box to act as a bar and it was the only cider outlet in the increasingly popular Haskins Field. I have known John for quite a few years now whist he has increased his production and storage capacity in his extended garage where he even has a small belt press. He stores much of his cider in new oak barrels and I love the distinctive oakiness of the taste. I would suggest that his dry ciders was one of my favourite of the year and I came across it in a few local pubs.

Ham Hill Ciders were in the food tent. Run by four enthusiasts who have other full time jobs they have been making some excellent ciders for the past couple of years as they increase their knowledge and capacity. I have come across them on Wells Market and other exhibitions. They seem to focus more on bottle sales rather than drught – though they have product available in bag in box.

Talbot Harris. I must confess I was quite surprised to see Charlie Harris at the Mid Somerset. After all he is from the south Coast of Dorset and very much unknown locally. For some reason the trade stand stewards had put him right near the popular Hecks and other producers. I understand that he was a bit disappointed at the level of sales he achieved – given the above factors I am not surprised – what local cider people are going to buy from a stranger situated between Hecks and Worley's.

Then there is my small local cider bar in the Heritage Marquee:

Copse House Cider. A Bob Chaplin produced cider from Dorset. Extremely good cider which is mentioned elsewhere. And thanks very much to Bobs wife Liz who helped look after the bar for much of the day. Bob is the Cider Steward in this tent as I am the Chief Steward for the whole tent.

Stones Bittersweet. Available in a few local pubs and odd shows this is Richie and my cider. Tasting really good at this time of year. Have kept it slightly drier than sometimes so we can enjoy drinking it. Unfortunately Richie had a bad bug and missed the whole event.

Blackmore Vale Cider. Alan Berry from Templecombe is an excellent cider maker and winner of many awards – he won the supreme champion cider today. He had been here in the morning and then went off to do tastings at one of his outlets – Kimber's Farm Shop near Wincanton. We had to ring him up and get him back so Bob Cork of Shepton Cider Mill, this year's show president, could present the award.

Tom Moon. I was really pleased to meet local youngster Tom Moon who makes his cider at home in Sticklinch near West Pennard on the way to Glastonbury. He had come along on the Saturday to help us set up and fully get involved. He is 19 and very keen to learn. He started helping the late Frank Naish with a bit of his cider making and the excellent Denis France sources some apples out of Tom's fathers orchards and has been encouraging Tom. He managed to win the dry class with his cider so an excellent start for him.

Harry's Cider. Harry Fry from Long Sutton along with his partner Alison Chapman and son Toby are amongst the most seen cider makers these days. Over the past five years their business has grown enormously. Harry's own father owns orchards that have provided apples to Taunton and Shepton. Harry himself learnt pruning from a master at Taunton and after a mixed farming career now seems to have settled on cider. He makes an excellent clean products with the fresh taste of Dabinett apples. He also makes a couple of very good bottled ciders including a Dabinett single variety which Richie and I had with our Christmas Dinner this year.

Another excellent cider make who came to the show to find out how his ciders had done was John Harris of **Westcroft** near Brent Knoll. It was good to see him looking fit again after a period of illness. His Janet's Jungle Juice sets a standard for farmhouse ciders. He strives to keep added sweetener to a minimum and hopes to retain some residual sweetness by repeated racking. Well worth going to buy some of his ciders if you are out that way.

Although not on the same scale as the Bath and West there is now serious cider content at the Mid Somerset Show. With producers, competition and heritage, often a Scrumpy and Western band it would seem every third member of the estimated 20,000 crowd at the show was holding a glass of cider. The Mid Somerset show is certainly part of 'finding good cider'.

Corton Denham – Scrumpy and Western and Somerset cider makers to visit

It is early September when we visit a cider 'festival' at the Queens Arms at Corton Denham. Tucked away in the beautiful and little visited lanes and hills south of the A303 and Cadbury Castle this is a high quality food pub which is also very comfortable to just go in and have a pint or two.

It always has a good range of beers and was amongst the first pubs where we came across the new generation craft beers. I had one of the best pints I have ever drunk in a pub there a couple of Christmases ago. Sloe Walker, a special brew from the excellent Moors Brewery. In over 40 years of drinking good beer that really was a standout pint! They have also made a point of stocking some good local ciders both in bottles and in bag in box.

For some reason- possibly backache – Richie was driving for a change which was probably just as well. Richie, Christine and I had arranged to meet James and Anais there They had been looking at a new car in Yeovil and this took them a more time than they expected so we spent a rather longer at the pub than we meant to.

The main reason for going was to see the Mangled Wurzels play. These are our favourite Scrumpy and Western Band. They are generally referred to as a Wurzels tribute band and true the majority of their set is based on Adge Cutler numbers – however they also include some of their own material and often it is difficult to know where one begins and the other ends. Dave, Kev and Frank are good performers and I have seen them driving on crowds of 1000's at bigger cider festivals in Bath and Bristol. The crowd sing along to Wurzels favourites like Blackbird or Combine Harvester and also some of their own numbers. I never forget the first time I saw them playing outdoors in December in the Shepton Mallet Market Square. I heard a very familiar tune from a children's TV programme featuring a postman and his cat. However the lyrics were now referring to the cider brand 'Scrumpy Jack' as a load of 'cac!'- whatever that is.

Their show stopper is the 'Tractor song' with the immortal lyric, 'I can't read and I can't write but it don't really matter. For I comes up from Somerset and I can drive a tractor!' The whole ethos of Scrumpy and Western summed up in one sentence. When you get 1,000 people singing this as I once saw at the Frome

Cheese Show with the beat just getting faster and faster it is an awesome sound. The other great thing about the Mangled Wurzels is that they are really nice local guys who are always willing to have a chat. Maybe slightly embarrassing as wherever they see me in a crowd they always point me out and give a good plug to my books – I love it really!

This festival was held in a side room at the Queen Arms and opened out to a courtyard with a large gazebo. When we were there I doubt if there were ever more than 50 people present. There was a bar that must have had ciders from at least eight different local producers. We sat talking to one of these John Lawrence who only lives about 400 yards down the road. He was there taking his very attractive young dog out for a walk – well it is a good excuse. He is someone I come across frequently and I really like his excellent oaky ciders.

Most of the other ciders came from some of the excellent established traditional Somerset makers. I thought this may be a good time to point out some of the places where you can really go and find good ciders – those that are open to the public and have something to offer as a visitor location.

Burrow Hill Cider up the lanes from the A303 at South Petherton is run by the incredible Julian Temperly. He is known by most people for his Cider Bus which has a key position in the Glastonbury Festival. He is also the chap who took on the British Government and the European Union and won, to gain permission to call his distilled cider 'Somerset Cider Brandy'. This is a real top end product which gains constant plaudits from food commentators. Alongside it he does an number of innovative blends which as Richie points out are along the lines of some of the quality ciders from the 17th century and the 'Golden Age' of cider when they were focused on trying to make cider for the gentry which was superior to wine. He is a busy man with some very famous daughters but during the summer I was amazed that he came up to talk a breakfast I was involved in at the Dunster Show. It was only to about 30 people but he came and spoke excellently.

The farm is well worth hunting out. There is an orchard trail through his wonderful orchards and you can see the giant stills they use to make the brandy. The shop is in traditional farm buildings and has a great atmosphere, a bit like Hecks in Street, but going beyond that. There is a room where the cider is stored in barrels and if you buy draught your containers will be filled from these. Julian is a great believer of the barrel as an image of cider. He is delighted when he sees children coming with their fathers who buy draught cider from wooden barrels. This perpetuates the tradition forward into the future. The shop also sells a range of his bottled ciders and the cider brandy. A must stop on any tour finding good cider.

Rich's Cider – not to be confused with Richie! At Watchfield near Burnham on Sea is another good venue for cider tourism. You park alongside their orchards which are reputed to be below sea level and walk past the apple washing pit and production facilities on your way to the shop. This is a large shop which sets out their full range of ciders – tasting is essential. This is a family concern. Jan Scott took over from her father Gordon Rich when he passed away about 20 years ago. Her two sisters, cousin Martin (the cider maker) and her husband and children are all very much part of the business.

Beside the shop is a small museum of bygone cider artefacts and a favourite old tractor that was synonymous with Gordon. Then across the yard is Jan's latest venture – a café restaurant serving some very hearty food. The Sunday roasts are extremely popular and booking is essential. At other times you can turn up and will be certain of a good welcome and good food.

Perry's at Dowlish Wake is another down the lanes venue – this time to the south of Ilminster. The Perry's have been here since before the Second World War and with my wife coming from Crewkerne and myself working in Chard for a spell this was a frequent location for me to go and buy cider. This business has developed considerably over the past few years. Grandmother is still around and Jon a local accountant has now retired and his orchards are his pride and joy. His son George is now the main cider maker. They have developed the buildings – where there was once was a shop in a semi-open barn you will now find at state-of-the-art bottling line which they use for their own excellent ciders and for other producers – their award winning Dabinett is one of my favourites. A barn that used to store a display of old farm hay waggons has now been turned into an excellent shop – tasting area – and café. The waggons are still located around the yard.

Across from the shop a low range of farm building include the wash pit, the old press and another museum of old cider and farming artefacts. You can also wander into the orchards just across the lane you came in by. A friend of mine recently went there for the first time and reported back to me how impressed he was with this set up.

Sheppy's at Bradford on Tone are now almost a large scale cider maker and their bottled product will be found in nearly all supermarkets. However it remains on the farm where is has been since early in the 20th century and the production remains true to proper cider principles. You can buy all descriptions of cider from draught through to a massive range of bottled ciders. This still includes the Exhibition, Goldfinch and Bullfinch brands that date back over 80 years along with ciders made with modern dessert varieties and a couple of different fruit ciders. The raspberry one is very popular but not for me – though I was impressed with the clean tasting blackberry and elderflower in which I did not find the added flavours overpowering.

Again you are encouraged to walk in their orchards – though some of this has now been lost through the recent building of their new factory. There is again a rural artefacts museum and a café – though here that has been franchised out as a separate business. David and his wife Louisa are very approachable people and have a high profile in the cider world. David has one of the best cider palettes I know. I resist giving him my cider to taste as I know it will never be up to his exacting standards!

One producer now operates out of their own pub. Jane and Michael Woods of **Woods Family Cider** run the excellent Lamb and Lion at Hambridge north of Ilminster. As well as good food and beer in the pub they serve their own very drinkable traditional cider and there is also separate cider snug.

There are many other cider makers where visitors are welcomed, most mentioned elsewhere in this book and where you are welcome to a tasting. To make sure I have covered them I would just list out **Hecks** in Street, **Bere Cider** near Aller, Nigel Stewart at **Bridge Farm** between Crewkerne and Yeovil, **Crossmans** at Congresbury. John Harris at **Westcroft** Brent Knoll, **Wilkins** at Mudgely near Wedmore. They are all working businesses and you may have to wait a while for someone to turn up. However, they are all worthwhile visiting. Please remember they are not there just to give away ciders – the purpose of tastings is to allow you to choose which one is to your taste so you can buy some! You wouldn't think you need to point this out but you do get reports of the occasional tourist who is happy to take up the cider makers time and taste his cider without any intention of buying!

Anyway this is just a few pointers on your journey to finding good cider.

Cider Making Displays

Come September and October there is a wonderful blossoming of interest in cider making. This is fuelled by the sight of cider apples on the trees and that wonderful experience of being in an orchard at this time of year. There is a huge community involvement feel about it with many events held in local orchards where children run around ineffectively picking up apples and bringing then to be crushed in a variety of hand powered scratters and presses and the sweet juice lovingly tasted by all but which the amateur cider makers present try to preserve as much as possible to take home to ferment to try to turn into cider.

A few of these displays in village orchards or city farms do occasionally lead to some cider which is bought out the following year. The nearby village of Pilton with Jo King has become very proficient at this and at another local village, Lamyatt, Nick Smallwood almost crosses into commercial production with his cider brand Bullbeggar cider with a good label with a folklore story on it.

It is great to see the enthusiasm that events like this engender more young people people into the orchards has to help continue the traditions for future generations.

It was seeing equipment for home cider making demonstrated by Vigo at the Bath and West Show that first made me intent on getting some equipment and having a go – even though being somewhat impecunious with a young family it was a decade or so before I actually bought any equipment. Vigo have recently split their business into professional equipment for the serious producers of cider wine or beer and the hobby equipment for the amateur or smaller scale artisan producer. For years Richie and I have straddled the two which may be a bit more difficult now. The smaller scale equipment side of the business has been sold off to a new company called Vigo Presses which now operates out of a unit across the road from the main business. It is now owned by Paul Courtney who owns one of the old Whiteway's cider orchards and got a prize at the Devon County show with his **Courtney's of Whimple** cider. He is joined at Vigo Presses by the long serving and delightful Amanda Farmer and Mavis. I know Amanda for her help to the Bath and West Cider committee and I recently discovered that her son's girlfriend is one of the daughters at **Henry's Cider** of Tanpits in Taunton. Given the huge amount of building in the area I was not sure Henry's Cider still existed but apparently it does and daughter and boyfriend have now taken it on. With an eye to opportunity I have suggested that Vigo Presses along with Henrys Cider could put on a demonstration in the Heritage Tent at the Mid Somerset Show. I strongly feel that this would be the right location for them to sell presses at the right time of year – just as the apples in people gardens are beginning to ripen and they are wondering what to do with them!

In the autumn of 2015 I got involved two very different demonstrations. The first was at the invitation of the interesting Ben Weller of Long Burton near Sherborne where we did a demonstration in Sherborne Museum.

Ben runs **Twisted Cider** and makes some traditional ciders from apples he collects in local orchards of which there are a surprising number in the south east corner of Somerset and into North Dorset where he operates. Ben tries to combine his cider business with working for the Civil Service and can only get home at weekends. He started trying to be a cider wholesaler but this would not fit in with work. He has built a very good press and the equipment to go with it and from a recent tweet I saw on Twitter he appears to now be trying to fabricate equipment for other producers. He is certainly a very energetic person!

I had not realised that there was a museum in Sherborne, but when you think about it, it is of course just the place that should have one. Tucked away at the bottom of town near the Abbey it is a delightful and well-presented museum where I was delighted to give a copy of my Dorset Cider book. Although like most local museums there was never a big crowd during the course of the morning we must have talked to and demonstrated to about 30 people. Probably there was a preponderance of the retired but there was also a healthy number of fathers with children under 12. Ben had prepared well. He chopped up the apples with a knife then put them a few at a time through a domestic kitchen juicer. He then put the pomace into a cheesecloth sock and with bare hands wrung it out! Much to my surprise he got sufficient quantities of juice for those who wanted it to have a taste. Simon and Victoria Baxter had provided a small bag in box of their very nice **Sherborne Cider** to provide some tastings of the finished product. Everyone there seemed to be entertained, educated and fully engaged.

I had to leave about lunchtime as I had to drop off a bag in box of our Stone's cider at the Travellers Rest at East Pennard on my way to watch Yeovil Town play fotball.

The other demonstration I was involved in was on a much larger scale. One of the Directors at Old Mill where I work lives in the village of Stoney Stratton near Evercreech. His mother in law Jane owns a wonderful cider orchard in the hamlet named Neale's Orchard after her late husband. For a couple of years now she has held an event in the orchard inviting the village. Local cheesemaker and relative Tom Calver of the award winning Westcombe Cheddar puts up a large marquee and a number of local cider enthusiasts bring their equipment down to use up some of the copious quantities of apples in the orchard. The occasion is of course also used to raise money for local charities.

Unfortunately the weather included some rather heavy showers but people did not really seem to notice. Fathers joined children in picking up apples and I think there were four different presses squeezing out juice and there were a lot of locals whom I have got to know over the years.

Tom Calver is an in interesting character. He farms with father Richard – who is one of the senior committee members at the Bath and West and was also present. Westcombe Cheddar is one of the three unpasteurised Cheddars which form part of a Slow Food Movement presidium along with Montgomory's and Keen's. The elite of British farmhouse Cheddar. Tom has always hankered after cider making – he made a lot for his own wedding a couple of years ago. He has a new Hydro press which I helped him get set up to use – it worked even though the water was coming from the house over 50 yards away! I hope that one day Tom will go a step further with his cider making. The tradition of West Country agricultural heritage is of small farms making both cider and cheese as part of their commercial diversity. Tom is just about the nearest to doing both that I have come across. However, cheese takes the commercial lead. He is currently constructing a huge 'cave' on their farm in which to mature their cheeses – an interesting and innovative move. I bought some cheese of him at the event.

He also has as tenants on his farm the Craft beer brewer Wild Beer. They make a range of top end craft beers and also have a beer in the marquee. We really are spoilt for choice

Anyway the community spirit is amazing despite the weather.

There are demonstration events like this now held across the country. 10 years ago the organisation Common Ground co-ordinated and promoted 'apples day'.

It took off to such a degree that it became self-sustaining and they withdrew to let it run its own course and it has continued to spread and build. Please look out for events like these in your own locality. It enhances and furthers the real meaning of 'finding good cider' and is essential if cider is not going to become solely identified as a pub and supermarket commodity.

The Perils of Perry – and a lot about the Three Counties

Let's start at the beginning. perry is not cider. The two products are frequently tagged together with perry relegated to either a poor brother status – or alternatively the wild esoteric edge of the subject. Indeed I am very guilty of that myself here with only passing references throughout the book. However this is certainly not intended to belittle the product.

Whereas cider is the fermented juice of apples – or should be – perry is the fermented juice of pears – or should be! At its best some people would rate perry above cider – especially as its slightly vinous taste can more easily lead to the comparisons with good wine which in the 17th century assumed significant debate. Unfortunately a some of the perry that made is virtually impenetrable.. The distinctive perry taste does not come through and you are left with a drink that makes some of the worst cider taste palatable.

For a small scale maker in Somerset we are very fortunate in having a small source of perry pears. Through my involvement with the Royal Bath and West Society I have permission to go and pick up some perry pears from a row of tree that would appear to have been planted in the 1990s, they also have a small orchard right inside the middle of the showground of trees planted in the 1960s which are considerably bigger. The important thing to understand is that these are proper perry varieties. Just as there are specific cider varieties of apples so there are of perry pears – indeed there would appear to be just as many varieties of perry pears as there are of cider apples, though in many cases there are only one or two trees of any one variety. Fortunately they are very long-lived trees which grow to an immense size. They are also renowned to take an excessively long time to start to bear fruit – 'you plant perry pears for your sons'. This may have contributed to the relative decline of the fruit during the modern age of intensive agricultural practice. Fortunately there has always been a hard core of interest. The Long Ashton Research Station near Bristol included perry pears within its remit for most of the 20th century and I know of one of their former specimen orchards still producing fruit. Recent years has seen more interest and a lot of trees have been propagated and indeed planted – usually on modern stocks which should see them bearing fruit before too long. The national collection of perry pear trees is held Hartpury College in Gloucestershire and is open to the public with tastings on a regular basis once a month. We have made some attempts to identify the varieties we have been picking up – there is an excellent book on perry varieties – but some many are so similar it really does need an expert to confirm them if you do not have access to the original planting plan!

The home of perry is in West Gloucestershire. In fact some people would suggest that it is not proper perry unless it has been made with pears grown within sight of May Hill – the only place where the trees are said to flourish. This would seem to deny the place name evidence spread across the South West. There are many Pear Tree Farms and other pear rooted field and place names which suggest a long history in both Somerset and Dorset – and probably much further afield if someone made the study.

Early October saw Richie and I armed with our sacks bending or kneeling under the row of perry pear trees on the Bath and West. Although there were many pears on the ground there were many more on the trees. It is one of the problematic enigmas of perry. Trees do not ripen at once but when the fruit is ripe it needs harvesting and pressing within days. The fruit rots from the inside so it is not immediately evident that fruit has gone over the top – and this can happen almost overnight. It makes it quite a difficult fruit to process. We only pick up about five or six sacks each year and make about 60 litres. Some years it has been absolutely marvellous – last years was not bad. However, in other years doing exactly the same thing we have produced perries to which to say the least are disappointing. One years we were the only entry at the Mid Somerset Show and failed to get a placing! Another year we had two perries one of which we were entering to the competition at the Bath and West. We chose the best of the two three days before the show and bottled it. The other we took down to give away as hospitality of the Old Mill marquee at the show. We were a bit disjointed not to get a place. I asked perry guru Tom Oliver who had been judging whether he had noted it. He didn't seem sure – he came over to our marquee and tasted the other perry and asked why we hadn't entered that perry as it was quite good! We were rather puzzled until we got the failed entry back and tasted it – it was awful – it had changed that much in a few days inside a sterilised airtight glass bottle!

Yes, perry is a very fickle drink but at its best is wonderful. We could, if we had time make more than our annual 60 litres but given the variety of results we prefer to keep it limited and mainly for our own consumption. Another interesting peril of perry is the time it takes to mature. In March we have perry which has fermented but tastes nondescript. In June we try again and sometimes it has been totally transformed with the perry perfume coming through strongly. In 2015 our perry still did not impress us in June – however by the Mid Somerset

Show in mid-August it was tasting pretty good and it was very popular at the Somerset Food and Drink Festival in mid-October.

Traditionally the biggest user of perry pears in Somerset used to be Showerings for their world beating perry – Babycham. Such was the immense marketing success of this product that few still realise it was basically an 8% strength perry. The drink that made it all right for women to drink in public and pubs was actually quite strong and traditional. Although Babycham is still made and bottled in Shepton Mallet, mainly for the Christmas market, its glory days have gone and all the orchards have been taken out.

There are still Somerset perry makers though. Perhaps the largest is Hecks of Street who have their own orchards and also get some from the Bath and West. They make a few single variety perries. The heavily perfumed Blakeney Red is one of my favourites – Hendre's Huffcap is a more subtle and sophisticated. Keith Balch of Piglets Cider has access to one of the old Long Ashton orchards and in recent years has made some wonderful ciders. In the Three Counties, Hereford, Gloucestershire and Worcester there is a wider choice however in general it is something you have to search out. It is very rare to find in pubs – and then only try it is it is in a bag in box. On the rare occasion I have seen it in the traditional five gallon brown barrel it is definitely worth avoiding!

As with 'good cider' there is also same spectrum when identifying what is good perry – are you getting a 100% perry juice artisan product – and does it matter?!

For a start – does it contain just the juice of perry pears? There is exactly the same argument – how much has it been watered down – it is very likely that the 'pear ciders' of the larger makers contain a low level of juice. But there is another complication on top of that. perry is apparently allowed to contain up to 30% apple juice – and conversely cider is allowed to contain up to 30% pear juice. How and who monitors this is very open to question and although you can see how it makes pleasant drinkable product I cannot see that it does anything but adulterate the subtle flavours of perry!

There is again the question of how much comes from concentrate. Yes, there is a big market in pear concentrate and it is probably even more the case than with ciders that the commercial products of the larger makers are solely using concentrate. I can remember interviewing Matthew Showering of Brothers drinks a few years ago. Brother's drinks are interesting – they do not claim to be making traditional products in traditional ways – their strength as a company for the past 20 years has been in bottling alchopops – so there cannot be the criticism that they are pretending to be something they are not. However Matthew, when explaining that a pear base in a drink holds added flavours better than apple did reveal that all their product was at that time made from 30% Spanish pear concentrate of mainly Conference pears. In the summer of 2015 they launched 'Mallets Cider (named after Shepton Mallet not the hammer). The media publicity talked about it being made to a traditional family recipe but it was evident that it was not being made in a traditional way.

There is also the question as to whether the perry is made with traditional perry pears or with dessert pears. I show my ignorance by being slightly less concerned about this than some other issues. Nigel Stewart of Bridge Farm Cider makes and sells a fair amount of what he refers to as 'Pear Cider' – and it is pretty good. However I know the orchard where in previous years he got his pears. It is all dessert varieties of pears, mainly Conference and Concorde. The first time Richie and I made 'perry' it was with some pretty unripe pears from a conference tree of a friend of ours. Much to our surprise it tasted all right – maybe the flavour was a bit too delicate but it had the distinctive taste we hadn't expected. Is this the equivalent of the so called 'eastern' style ciders? It could be, but as in cider they appear to lack the complexity and depth of flavour. Perry is an drink where I am still trying to expand my knowledge and palette!

Sweetness is another peril with perry. Most of the commercially available 'pear ciders' are extremely sweet alcopop type drinks. Based on the current fashion for very sweet products 'pear cider' has been identified as a sweet drink and a lot of the products available are too sweet. In good perries this is complicated by the fact that unlike cider – which naturally ferments our dry and has to have sweetness added back in – when perry pears are used a proportion on the sugars in the juice are sorbitol, a non-fermentable sugar. This often leaves a pleasant residual sweetness in the finished product. It is also responsible for the laxative effect which can be part of drinking real perry!

I have left to last the sometimes heated debate concerning to the term 'pear cider'. Cider is a fermented drink made of apples – perry a fermented drink made of pears. The definitions strongly suggest the idea of a pear-based drink being any kind of cider is a total misnomer. Much as I dislike the alcopops like 'Strawberry Cider' at least it is usually an apple based drink even if it has sickenly sweet strawberry syrup added to it.

The term pear cider is something the marketing men have taken up in the past ten years. It may have come from the Brother's Bar at successive Glastonbury Festivals where they have for many years sold their 8% perry. Perhaps they got fed up with trying to explain to people the 'perry is like cider but made with pears' and started referring to it as pear cider. In the past 10 or so years the marketing men around the commercial cider giants have taken the phrase up and the reality is that by dumbing down it has now become a generally accepted term.. Let's keep 'perry' for the really interesting stuff made from special perry pears and by people who make it for the love of it. Finding 'good perry' will hopefully remain a task for the discerning few – though that few should be a good many more than the very few it is at the moment!

October 3rd - A day of finding real good cider

Saturday the 3rd October was a grey dull day but one on which Richie and I set off for one of our best finding good cider (and perry) days of the year.

I spotted a random tweet about a cider pressing at the Yew Tree Inn at Peterstow in south Herefordshire at which the Skimmity Hitchers would be playing. Having had a chat with Dave of the Skimmities only a few weeks earlier at the Frome Show I was keen to go and see if there was more to them than my initial impressions.

Try as I might I could find no information about the event. I even checked the Skimmities web site and although they were playing in Reading the night before supporting the Wurzels, with whom they share management, the Yew Tree event was not mentioned. However, about two days before I checked again and the event was now up. So I persuaded Richie it would make a nice trip, after all it is only about one and half hours' drive (nearer two actually) and if we stopped there for a hour or so we could be back by mid-afternoon. Where cider is concerned timekeeping is never one of my stronger attributes.

You will recall that we had discovered the Yew Tree when we dropped in on our way back from a long weekend in Shropshire much earlier in the year. I had come across Mike Johnson of Ross on Wye Cider when he still operated out of Broome Farm a couple of years ago and I had always been impressed by both the man and his cider – and perry. However distance does not make it easy to develop relationships. After a drive which took just that bit longer than expected, Richie and I parked in the pub car park and wandered through to the Cider shop in a new shed out the back. This had been brand new when we first dropped in. After the drive getting a glass of cider was the first thing on our agenda. Mike recognised me straight away and much to my delight asked if I had any more of my books with me as they seemed to be selling in the shop. Unfortunately I hadn't many on the car and with stocks of the most relevant 'In search of cider' dwindling it will probably be this book that I provide him with next.

Behind the bar in the shop there where three dry ciders in 1,000 bag in boxes on offer. Each a slightly different but wonderful tasting blend. One from a particular orchard – the others blends of cider varieties. These were wonderful – I am trending to the direction of them being my favourite ciders of the year. Glasses in hand we wandered out to take a look around the event.

Just outside the cider shop there was a stage on a farm trailer on which the Skimmity Hitchers were testing the sound. This was at one end of a relatively small paddock around which were a good number of stands and displays and a reasonable number of people. As we walked around we suddenly came across a face that was very familiar to me – but only through television. We started talking to the extremely distinctive Pete Symonds. He was dressed as I had seen him on TV on an episode of I think it was Hugh and Oz Drink to England. He informed us that he was dressed as 'The Butler'. In Gloucestershire it would appear that this is an essential character in wassail – the master of ceremonies. As a student of wassail who has frequently taken on the role of Master of Ceremonies myself I was delighted to discover him. He had prepared a leaflet 'Everything you need to know about a wassail. And published it from an organisation known as CROW – the Campaign for the Revival of Wassail. A campaign very much after my ownheart and I was delighted to have a good chat with him. There were some interesting slight differences between the Somerset Wassail and the Gloucester one – other than just the role appearance of the Butler. The date for a start – his pamphlet says in should be Old Christmas Day, the 6th of January, whereas most follow the idea of it being Old Twelfth Night eve, the 17th of January.

These are minor points of difference and his leaflet will add a valid contribution to my rather limited collection of publications about wassail – the amazing 'Seasons of the Sun' by Professor Ronald Hutton – under whom Richie studied and still works with at Bristol University and 'Wassailing, The British Midwinter Blessing Custom' by Simon Reed. It is really part of the tradition of many local customs that there is no right way of doing it as customs evolved in different locations mainly before the age of mass communication. However, the similarity in words and tune or the wassail songs does suggest that these may well be 18th century with a common source. The fact that I think the origins of wassail is much more recent than the Pagan Tradition that some suggest I have covered in previous books.

The wassail that I remembered the Butler leading in the Hugh and Oz programme was however very special. It had obviously been staged for the benefit of the cameras. I suspect it may have been raining outside. I am not sure what other reason there could have been for bringing a potted apple tree about three feet tall indoors and holding the ceremony around it! The tradition of wassailing the biggest tree in the orchard conveniently side stepped. It is wonderful what television producers will get people doing.

However, I was really delighted to meet Peter whose face I had distinctly remembered from the programme probably three years before. In our discussions with him we were lubricated with a sample of a cider he had made which we were asked to identify, It was very pleasant but the high acidity gave it away as a Bramley apple cider – these are such an accessible apple and so easy to work with it is one we have been tempted to make – even though we know it is never going to make anything other than a rather sour cider.

Just round the corner of the paddock a fairly large cheese was being build up on a traditional rack and cross hydraulic press. The mill and elevations were being run by delightful popping stationary engines. This is an outfit that is demonstrated by Albert Wrixon and I think when the full set up is there the press is worked by a steam engine with a boiler. Albert is one of the real characters of cider in Gloucestershire – and indeed all over the cider making area. A large man with a lazy eye and very much the appearance of a country yokel he is a familiar and welcome sight. I had last seen him demonstrating his press opposite the cider tent at the Bath and West Show where the area became a welcome resting place for many of the more traditional West Country cider makers. Albert also makes some extremely good ciders himself. A couple of years ago, at the Powerstock Cider Festival, he gave me a taste of a three year old Keeved cider he had made. It was one of the richest and most complex tasting ciders it has ever been my honour to drink.

It was from him that I discovered the genesis of the today's event. In previous years there has been a steam and cider event in Hampshire at the home of New Forest Cider where Albert and others have teamed up with Barry Topp and his family to put on a weekend with an awesome reputation. However it had grown and grown and the previous year the success of the event had led to problems of scale. This year they had decided to have a rest and Albert had talked to Mike Johnson about holding this smaller event at the Yew Tree. This was very much an experiment. Mike has for many years run a weekend camping cider event in August down the lane at Broome Farm. This is another event that has proved so popular it has outgrown its comfortable origins and the growth of interest in cider has led to Mike moving much of his cider business up to the Yew Tree. This latest event was only billed as a cider pressing demonstration and as mentioned earlier the publicity had been very limited. Mike was particularly worried about the limited size of the car park, close to a main road, and the fact that the paddock was quite small. In the event although it had a good crowd and atmosphere I doubt if there were ever more than 200 people on the site during the afternoon. In fact talking to Mike I got the feeling that he would really have liked more people to make it economically viable.

Another participant from the New Forest event was Dom White from Dorset – in fact there was a bit of a Dorset theme to the day. I was a bit concerned when I first saw the sign 'Dom White Cider – Dorset. I naturally assumed it may have been a producer I had missed out of my 2014 book Dorset Cider. I needn't have worried. He was a really nice guy who was another of the agricultural machinery heritage enthusiasts, interested in the actual pressing and its accompaniments. Yes he makes cider – but it is mainly for the consumption of himself and his friends. This is a crucial part of the 'good cider scene', and links in nicely with the Dorset tradition of cider ' sheds'. All across West Dorset and into Somerset, Devon and even Cornwall there is the tradition of local farmers and their friend – or even just the friends, getting together to make cider in the autumn and to consume on a regular basis on sociable evenings and weekends through the year. These are people who are really keeping the 'good cider' tradition alive and well.

It is about now that the Skimmity Hitchers played their first set. Until now I had been lukewarm about the Skimmities as the new wave of Scrumpy and Western Having met Tommy Banner and Pete Budd of the Wurzels through my father along with Shag O'Conner and the Carrot Crunchers and being quite friendly with the Shepton based Mangled Wurzels tribute band I had not looked much further. I had seen the Skimmity Hitchers a couple of times before at the Powerstock Cider Festival. I had chatted to the stocky and smiling double bass player Dave as he is married to the best friend of my close colleague Kim who has worked with me at marketing Old Mill for over seven years. However my impression was that they were a very loud, fast and very rude wall of sound that rather hurt my eardrums.

Seeing them outside playing a farm trailer Richie and I were about to have our ideas very much shaken up. We can only put our previous impressions down to the acoustics in the Powerstock Village Hall where you are stuck in a dense press of people with the sound reverberating off a very low ceiling.

Here on a trailer stage and out in the open things were very much transformed. Yes they were loud and fast and very rude and it was wonderful. This was Scrumpy and Western in the raw. Driven by Dave on double base, Jack on guitar the amazing Kev on lead vocals backed by a drummer they put on a performance which was really exciting. Cider orientated vocals, a strong sense of place from South Dorset it was both exciting music and hilarious humour – now I could hear the words. They largely followed in the Wurzel tradition of adapting old favourite tunes with new lyrics which transcend the originals and get you dancing and laughing.

For the purpose of earning a living they have had to leave Dorset and now work in Bristol. Some of them are family men but in the past couple of years the band have latched on to the cider revolution and are now capitalising on a rapidly growing reputation. As I mentioned earlier, last night they had been supporting the Wurzels at an event in Reading and they share their management for arranging suitable gigs. In the New Year they have hope to be performing a few gigs in America around a cider conference. This book will not be out until after they return but I have a feeling the Americans with their own huge cider making revolutions now gaining great pace will just lap them up – though they may have to clarify a lot of their humour. Explaining that Portland in Dorset is not the same place as Portland Oregon may be a good starting place.

Anyway that first set not only sold us on their music, but meant we were certainly not going to leave before they had played their other two sets. We were not going to be back home for the mid-afternoon. We were there for the duration.

Feeling hungry, we had to get something to eat. Richie being a vegetarian we had to get a cheese ploughmans for him from the pub. I however headed straight for the stand doing Broome Farm lamb burgers. I was first introduced to good lamb burgers by the Thoroughly Wild Meat Company who are based at the Bath and West Showground and whose Salt Marsh Lamb Burgers are a taste experience to savour. The Broome Farm lamb burgers did not let me down – so good was my first burger that I had to have another.

Continuing our sipping of halves of cider we used the gaps between sets to have a good look at some more of the stands. One was the display promoting the Hartpury Orchard Centre. Hartbury College is one of the local agricultural colleges and strongly connected with cider and perry. Richie had spent a week there when he did a cider making course under Peter Mitchel about five years previously where he had learnt the disciplines that have enabled us to become reasonably proficient (views vary!) cider makers. He certainly learnt to far outstrip my previous haphazard attempts. Hartpury Orchard Centre contains the National Perry Pear Collection with over 100 varieties of perry pear. This is a valuable resource to help ensure the survival of these varieties and to help propagate fresh trees for the future and to replace some of the ancients trees as they age and find their position in the countryside under threat. The orchard also contains a number of old Gloucestershire varieties of cider apples. The orchard is open for people to walk around every day of the year except Christmas. I am afraid it is not somewhere I have been yet – and when I do I want to make sure it is on one of the Saturday afternoons once a month when there are reputed to be tastings.

The stand promoting it was absolutely fascinating. Being the harvest time of year there was a wide number of different perry pears on display. As mentioned before we have access to some varieties of perry pears in Somerset to make a small amount for our own use. We are used to seeing the variety of shapes and colours but I don't think I was quite prepared for the variety on display today. The smartest perry pears are pear shaped – though considerably smaller than any pears you would be tempted to buy in the shop. Their colour transfuses from a bright light yellowy green through to a blush of red – Blakeney Red fits this description and along with a number of other varieties look quite attractive. Many of the other varieties seem to be even smaller, slightly more spherical than you would usually associate with pears, thought they do have the distinctive pear stalk. They are mainly dull green to russet brown and do not exactly look tempting. In fact I have yet to find a perry pear which really pays for the effort to taste them. They are rather like biting into wood with evidence of heavy tannins. Cider apples are unpalatable enough but perry pears surpass them in lack of pleasant texture and taste by a country mile. Here, also on display, were many other varieties which I had not seem before including, I think it was, the 'potato pear'. You can only say many of these varieties defy and describable shape - amorphous lumps. However the magic of perry is that from these comes an amazingly rich pallet of tastes – when they are got right. As I have already alluded to perry as a bit of a mystery and it takes considerable experience – plus the right fruit and conditions and the right timing for them to release their magic.

In the corner of the field is the Vintage van promoting Charles Martell's distilled spirits and believe it or not the man himself. This is the first time I have met Charles and I was thankful for Pete Symonds – still dressed as the Butler – for introducing me. He was a very pleasant quietly spoken chap who in our conversation exuded a mastering of knowledge around cider and perry which was a pleasure to hear. He is responsibility for two amazing comprehensive books on the perry pears and cider apples of Gloucestershire. These substantial tomes would appear to easily outweigh the excellent efforts of Liz Copas in Somerset, Dorset, Devon and Cornwall. This is a heritage under threat and it is fantastic that someone has made the study. The books were available on the Hartpury stand. I am going to need to save up – at around £30 each they are not an impulse purchase.

Charles is a major figure in artisan food and drink. He has been making his perry based spirit drinks in a still since 2010 and they have won wide acclaim. However it as the saviour of Gloucester cattle and a renowned cheese maker that he is best known. About six weeks after this I bumped in to him again judging at the World Cheese awards at the NEC Birmingham. In the 1970s he was instrumental in bringing the then endangered Gloucester cow back from the brink of extinction. This rather bony looking dairy cow with a white stripe along its back is one of the few remaining regional dairy breeds that would have been commonplace early in the 20th century before the introduction of the black and white cows. Its milk has small fat globules which make it particularly suitable for cheese. He became an artisan cheese maker on his small Gloucestershire farm and reintroduced the Single Gloucester Cheese. In the early 1990s he developed a new soft cheese, Stinking Bishop, which has won numerous awards. It is known as one of the countries smelliest cheeses but actually has quite a mild but complex taste. The secret comes from the curds being washed with perry giving a distinctive aroma and taste. Stinking Bishop is the name of the perry pear variety from which the perry for this process is made.

Charles Martell and Son now make seven different cheeses – as their web site says that is plenty for one farm. They have out stripped the supply of milk from their Gloucester cattle, though the breed is now well on the way to being secure.

However, despite the obvious potential the business has remained a relatively small family affair – he is a definite champion of the artisan producer and a focus on quality.

The afternoon crowd was never the throng it might have been but it was extremely well supported by the three counties cider fraternity. There were a number of people who I knew well by sight but could not put a name to. One who I could name was cider and perry guru and tour manager for the evergreen Proclaimers, Tom Oliver, who was as genial as ever and introduced me to a number of other people. Richie and I made out way baiek to the shop and we looked at the wall of numerous varieties of bottled perries and iders from Ross on Wye Cider. Mike Johnson specializes in small batches of particular varieties or blends. We could not take them all back. We selected Balls Bitter Sweet Cider, Browns Apple Cider, Ellis Bitter Cider and we could not resist the Michelin Cider. Michelin is one of the most widely grown cider apples in the cider makers' commercial orchards. However, it has a name as being a 'bulker' so we were interested to see what had been made of it as a single variety in its own right. When we later tried it we found a well-made cider with a good flavour but it has to be admitted was a bit on the 'thin' side to be of real note.

From the amazing range of bottled perries, I am sure n -one makes a wider variety, we selected Gin Pear Perry, Red Perry and a Brockhampton Blend Sparkling Perry made from traditional varieties found in a particular Brockhampton orchard which was very nice. After persuading Mike that we had to pay for some of the bottles, we packed these in the car before watching the Skimmity Hitchers last set of the day which maintained the zest and enthusiasm they had started with many hours before.

Richie and I drove back down the M5 listening to our recently purchased collections of the Skimmities CD's – a bulk purchase of three for £20. It had been such an interesting and enjoyable day. A real finding good cider day..

Cider History

I would say I am a reasonably serious cider historian – though others would suggest I merely observe and write journalistic reports on the industry.

With the background of a degree in Economic and Social History and an interest in rural history I can trace back to school days I have been fascinated in rural history for a long time now.

Cider History is very much part of that and I have read most of the 17th and 18th century treatises and looked at all the reports from Long Ashton and more. However I fully admit that working full time I have not yet had the time to apply the scholastic rigours that are necessary. Nearly all that has been written in the past century on cider history is very impressionistic and no one done the research work necessary to write a full history.

'Maybe when I retire' has been my creed for a long time – but retirement does not seem to get closer as I work harder and harder. Anyway I appear to have been usurped by my own son, Doctor Richard Stone, a teaching fellow at Bristol University in Early Modern History. Although Pirates, Smuggling, Slavery and Drink and Disorder are his core topics he has also along the way put in effort around cider. You can see him on YouTube in a video about the Golden Age of Cider with TV historian Sam Willis, he was also recently on the BBC Today programme talking about the development of cider tree varieties and I had a shock a couple of weeks ago when as a CAMRA member I opened my latest copy of their newspaper 'What's Brewing' and there was Richie's face beaming out at me from the back page. He has also been invited to speak on cider history at a number of conferences – the latest at Cambridge University. He has promised me a 3,000 word article to include in this book.

However, all this does not stop me being interested in a piecemeal way in cider history. I still write articles and stage cider heritage displays both at the Bath and West Show and at the Mid Somerset Show. Often I find it nice when you come across something in small bites. I was delighted this week when at an Old Mill farmers meeting a friend from the Bath and West Show, Allan Cotton, handed me an envelope with a couple of bits he had come across in his paperwork.

The Allen element of his name comes from the W T Allen family from West Bradley. Allen still lives on one of their local farms. The Allen's used to be based at West Bradley House and planted the orchards now owned by Edward Clifton Brown. They were certainly apple growers in a big way – you still come across a lot of apple crates with their name stamped on them. They were heavily involved in the introduction of the Friesian breed of cows into this country in the 1930s and they also made cider.

With a warm sense of anticipation at breakfast the next morning I pulled the first of the two documents out. It was 'First Report on 1943 Apple Crop' for the National Association of Cider Makers. They still gather information for this report today at NACM. It covered the country with short reports. For instance

'Mr G H Pallett, Taunton Cider Company, Norton Fitzwarren, states it is too early to give anything like a reliable estimate of the apple crop prospect. He further states the blossom was excellent but encountered dramatic weather, and most orchards in this area have suffered severely from blight. There is however no reason to suppose that the crop will be less than last year and he anticipates a slightly heavier one.'

While just down the road from the Allen's

'Mr R Clapp of Glastonbury reports that will be somewhere about half a normal crop in his area. The cold winds have severed the trees badly in this area.'

Even today cider orchardists watch the weather with a deep obsession to see what effect it will have on their yield of apples. It is one of the perennial fascinations of cider. You can't beat the weather.

The other document I pulled out was a folded report inside a small letter envelope printed 'University of Bristol, Agricultural and Horticultural Research Station, Long Ashton Bristol.' The envelope had a George V stamp on it and the postmark revealed a 1918 date.

It was a 'summons' to attend the Fifteenth Annual Meeting. The history of Long Ashton I have covered in previous books and elsewhere. But it is interesting what snippets you can pick up. Item 6 on the agenda

'To pass a vote of thanks to Right Hon. H. Hobhouse of the Governors, and Mr H.B.Napier, Chairman of the Managing Committee, and the Hon. Treasurer for their past services.

The Hobhouse referred to was a former owner of the orchards I went to see now owned by Alison and Mark Tilley.

Napier was the squire at East Pennard, a small village just to the south of Shepton Mallet which still has a lot of orchards run by Suzie Deardon – a descendent. I had written a fair amount about Mr Napier and his role as a magistrate in a previous book I wrote on the history of 'Silas. The Victorian Rural Postman.' Sometimes it is an amazingly small world even in history.

The report itself show that the Institute was now stable as it was being run totally by Bristol University.

It shows that the Institute was founded by the following bodies

The Board of Agriculture and Fisheries

The Bath and West and Southern Counties Society

Devon County Council

Gloucester County Council

Hereford County Council

Monmouth County Council

Somerset County Council

Worcester County Council

It then adds cryptically. ''and is in receipts of annual grants in aid of its work from each body with the exception of Hereford County Council.'

The report covers the distribution of the apple trees they had grown. Discussions with the French about the possibility of importing apples from France if the crop was poor and experiments with making apple jelly when there was a surplus crop.

It was also interesting to see that the annual tasting day was already established and popular. In the 1930s and 1950s this was a major event/session which is still well remembered by some.

Another thing I discovered was that the Bristol University member on the board was a Mr Hiatt Baker. When I was at Bristol, Hiatt Baker Hall was the newest of the University's student halls of residence for students. Somehow I had never before associated the name of the hall with a person!

Looking a snippets of history like this brings you so much closer to the heritage of cider and an understanding of the past and its relationship to the present. To me this is very much part of finding good cider.

Last year's Bath and West bought me into contact with another element of cider history. The pomologist Liz Copas always puts on a display alongside mine under the title of Long Ashton Research station – although it is now nearly 20 years since it closed its doors for the last time. She has a good archive. During the show Les Davies OBE gave me a contact name of another ex-Long Ashton employee, Bob Hughes, who still has many of pictures and documents from Long Ashton which he was looking to pass on. I arranged to go and visit him. He is a former worker at Long Ashton though not on the cider side. He was the last man standing and supervised the final closing of the Cider and Fruit Institute. He still lives overlooking the former orchards and his son is the tenant farmer of the former land which is still owned by Bristol University though they only seem interested in selling it for residential development.

We went to a reasonably modern farm building where inside on a table and above an office were two massive piles of maps, pictures, plans, records etc relating back to Long Ashton which he hadn't had the heart to throw out and is now looking for a responsible home for. Liz had already part sorted a small part of this and used it as part of her display at the show.

Bob seemed to accept my suggestion that the Bath and West Archive would be the right place for the long term future of these documents – they already have professionally managed archives. In early April 2016 he got the records over to the Bath and West and we are now planning to have some sessions to sort it and use some of the surviving employees to identify the photographs.

Bob Cork, Master Cidermaker

I had an excellent good cider evening with Bob Cork – cider master. I had felt the need for this journal to have a discussion from some-one who came from the large scale side of cider making. I have mentioned before that I certainly do not want to divide cider into good and bad, artisan/craft and industrial. There is good and bad cider on both sides of the fence – I just want to understand it more from the view point of someone who is passionate about cider having has spent a career working in a very large cider factory.

In this so far ridiculously mild winter it was pleasant to feel a touch of chill in the air. According to the car thermometer the temperature outside was down to one degree – though not quite touching a frost. Farmers, orchardists and gardeners could really do with a week of very hard frosts to kill off some of the population of bugs and pests which build up and help prepare for a fruitful season in the summer. There still seems no prospect of this and nature is currently rather muddled into thinking spring is already upon us. There are already worries that following the really bumper crop of apples last year there could be shortages this coming summer.

I met Bob at the Hunters Lodge Inn near Priddy on the top of the Mendip Hills which is Bob's local. It is a fascinating pub which has a very long serving landlord. Rather bleak and weather worn from the outside inside you find three old fashioned rooms with coal fires and a bar with some good beers served direct from cask. The first time I had come here about 20 years ago had been after a Round Table caving trip on Mendip and we ate our meal very late. It is a pub that despite its isolated position has a popular local following and is also the main haunt of the many cavers whose mission in life is to explore the insides of the Mendip Hills.

I discovered that Bob himself has been a very keen caver ever since his teenage days and has done a lot of teaching to aspiring cavers. Alongside his youthful passion was also a passion for diving, the two things meet in exploring underground rivers. He comes from Bristol and his passion for diving led to him joining underwater search teams searching for drowned body's whist he should have still been in school. He wanted to get on a professional divers course but that was a financial commitment well beyond his means. His best chance was getting a diving company to sponsor it – but to do that he had to have a recognised trade which would be useful for a company employing divers. This was in the days when we were building a lot of oil rigs for the North Sea so welding seemed a very sensible choice to train for.

It was a four year apprenticeship and he did a lot of welding all around the country in all industries including brewing and dairy. He then moved out to eastern Mendip to be close to his beloved caves where he did some work in the quarries. He went for an interview at the Shepton Cider Mill – then owned by Allied Breweries but with the Showering family influence still very strong. He discovered a mill where a lot of cider was still moved around in plastic pipes. The age of stainless steel was upon them and quite late in the day cider was following food production and brewing down the road of raising standards. There was plenty of scope for a young welder and at 22 Bob had arrived at the place where he would spend well over 35 years rising through the ranks to become a senior manager within the business.

Bob quite soon became the manager of the section milling the apples – the first stage of the operation, milling the apples into the mash for the presses. This was still very much an engineering based operation but Allied 'sent him back to school' and as a chap with potential he studied many things from process engineering to cider making to business management.. He fully believes that to be an engineer you need to have a full understanding for the products you are making. The Showering and Allied philosophy was to encourage talented people, especially in cider making. Most of the people who ended up in senior positions came up through the company. This has gone on until recent times with courses for professional cider making qualifications open to all being held at the mill. Many of the better of the new generations of cider makers like Barny Butterworth (Sandford Orchards) and Martin Berkeley (Pilton Cider) having been through this training – the legacy will be with us for at least another generation.

Bob moved up to be Mill and Fermentation Manager and as time moved on to become Factory Manager for the whole site. By the mid-1990s, whatever the ownership of the business three people had come to the fore. Maurice Cox and the two Bobs, Chaplin and Cork. Maurice was keen on local marketing and developed the very close relationship between the cider mill and the Bath and West Show. He is still lives locally but retired about ten years ago. Bob Chaplin spent over 40 years in the company starting in the laboratories and later looking after the company orchards and the many growers with contracts with them. In about 2012 in his late 50s he went down to four days a week and found himself spending the fifth working for a city businessman, Oliver Tant who was planting orchards in north Dorset and wanting to build a top end craft cider making business. Bob retired from the Shepton Mill and took over running the fledgling company full time in 2014. Their cider 'Copse House' cider has already won the Bath and West show competition.

Bob Cork's was the General Manager and Head of Production at Shepton Mallet involved in a lot of the due diligence work around the C&C take over. He was later elevated to Head of Product Development for the C&C Group covering their portfolio of products from soft drinks to beer and including cider of course. To successfully launch a major brand is reputed to cost around £20m. C&C showed willing and came up with some very interesting and innovative products although Magners was always their pole brand. One new product was an Italian cider with specific apples grown in a particular area, One of the best products they have come up with in recent years was their bottled premium 'craft' cider aptly named 'Chaplin and Cork'. Bob and I spent the evening sipping bottles of this excellent cider in the Hunters Lodge as our conversation wandered around the attributes of cider. One thing that has always been clear to me is how passionate the Bobs and many other employees at Shepton Cider Mill are about their products. They all drink them, they are all striving to make the best ciders in the world.

Both Bobs had become important figures in the world of Cider involved with the National Cider Makers Association (NACM) which without them would have looked rather Hereford and Bulmers focused. Bob Chaplin has also been the driving force behind the South West Cider makers Association (SWECA). Bob Cork became chair of the technical committee at NACM and sits on the Policy and Advisory Committee – the national body on cider production.

What makes good cider?

The conversation moved on to our main topic for the evening – what makes 'good cider'? Bob starts from the wider view point – one that I am in broad agreement with, but with some reservations. He feels that cider is very much driven by market forces and what the consumer wants to drink. He says they could produce an excellent Kingston Black single variety cider but that the wider public would not necessarily want to buy it. In the past decade their most successful new brand in Shepton Mallet was Gaymers Original (okay that is an old name but this was a new cider). This was softer and slightly sweeter than their traditional Blackthorn brand. It was available in keg but its main impact came through to 568 ml (1 Pint) bottles served over ice which sold in vast numbers in pubs & nightclubs. It fitted what the younger public were looking for and was building quite a head of steam particularly at Music Events & Festivals. Because of the similar brand proposition to Magners, Gaymers was later restyled to take advantage of the emerging fruit cider market and lost ground in its apple and pear cider roots

Bob feels that as cider makers large and small you have to go with the flow of changing markets if you want to remain profitable. However, he acknowledges that there are things that can be done in this area to lead with the unique position that genuine apple ciders and perries hold. Cider should not go with the lowest common denominator. When Shepton was part of Allied Domeque they were part of the biggest wine merchants in the world and the public have definitely been educated into a taste for different wines over the past 40 years. Bob feels there is a lot that can be learnt from the wine industry about marketing quality ciders – but points out that cider is not wine and is currently appealing to a very different drinking occasion In the UK cider is a long drink and is served as such even when accompanying food. Here I would diverge from him to a certain extent but largely agreeing with him that it not economically feasible for large scale cider makers to develop premium niche products with an initially small market. It is improbable that individual cider makers can alone tackle the sugar craving that the public currently has.

Marketing aside Bob feels that what makes a good cider is down to a few key factors – some of which will come as a bit of a surprise.

1) Good fruit – the basic raw material of the cider. Contrary to the perception of some of the fans of good cider this is crucial. One of the most important people from a large scale producer is adamant that 'good cider' cannot be made with just any old fruit but can be made from most apples provided they carefully selected for purpose. He cites the US cider market which is supposedly going through a big boom and massive innovation at the moment. Bob feels that given the preponderance of desert fruit in their ciders – and in particular the Mackintosh Apple

variety with is distinctive toffee apple taste. The majority of the base ciders in the US taste similar and are more one dimensional in their character. Work is proceeding with some cider makers to increase the use of bittersweet apples in their blend to produce more complex ciders. Other innovation and attempts to develop differentiated products therefore comes from adding other things and flavours – fruit ciders, spice ciders, hop ciders and more. I have heard some respected people in the British cider makers suggest that this is the way forward and that US may jump the apple cider phase.

Although what the Americans are in fact lacking is Bitter Sharp and Bitter Sweet fruit – high tannin fruit. In Britain we can make varied and distinctive ciders/perries through the blend of the wide varieties of apples and pears we have available. Bob says you can work out what a cider will taste like by going around an orchard and using a penknife to taste the apples. The variety of apples combined with the soils and growing conditions in Somerset gives us some of the world's very best cider fruit. This is a key factor to producing 'good cider.'

2) Bob also stresses that the timing of the harvest and production is major factor. To produce the best ciders the cider apples need to be ripe when they come into the mill. In the ripening process the starches in the apples get converted into sugars. The apples need to be harvested when sufficient starch has been naturally converted to sugars. The right timing varies very much from year to year and of course very much from variety to variety. Although people are always anxious to get started with their cider making the correct timing is probably later than some suspect – except for specific varieties like Morgan Sweet. October and November are more likely to be the right season. New varieties of Cider apples are trying to spread this season but there is still little experience with working with them.

Conversely it is also important that the apples have not got over ripe, desiccated or started to rot. There are certain undesirable faults that can get into cider that come from using fruit that has got over ripe and is in poor condition.

3) Selecting the right yeast and ensuring that this is consistent. One of the key aims of the larger scale cider makers and even the bigger artisan producers is that they have, within reason, consistent products. Consumers grow accustomed to a particular taste and do not want to expect one taste and receive another. I remember at a dinner one night the keg of a national brand cider that had been tasting particularly good ran out. The next keg was put on and I was made aware by a friend that it tasted totally different. It was greatly inferior. National brands try to avoid this at all costs. There are some small scale cider producers who believe in allowing the natural wild yeasts to dictate the fermentation. Even for our own ciders Richie and I have gone well beyond that. You have to produce product that people want to drink and consistency is a big part of that and it can in part be achieved by using selected and controlled yeasts.

4) Temperature control during fermentation. This is again to ensure consistent and repeatable product and taste. At the risk of showing my previous ignorance I had assumed temperature control was about heating the cider to get a faster fermentation and that this was a bad thing compared to a natural fermentation at ambient temperatures that lasts all the winter. However, I discovered from Bob that it is much more about taking heat out. The activity of the yeast during fermentation generates heat and the temperatures of the cider can build from an acceptable 23 degree centigrade up into the low 30s. There is a risk that at these temperatures the yeast will die and therefore the juice needs to be cooled during fermentation if a repeatable consistent process is to be achieved

There are also similar risks to ciders receiving a 'cold shock' during production. On occasions with ciders being produced with natural yeasts and low nutrient fruit in cold cider cellars the yeast can die and drop to the bottom of the vat. When the temperature heats up the remaining yeasts will slowly start the fermentation going again. This can lead to some wonderful ciders with a lot of residual sweetness. However there is also a much bigger risk of spoilage organisms getting in or the fermentation being taken over by very different yeasts. The exact conditions are not re-creatable for future ciders – this is not the way to go to get consistency.

This will come as a bit of a shock to many small 'craft' cider makers. They do not mind if one barrel tastes totally different to the next. They sing the praises of 'natural' methods of cider making and decry any product where they feel the process has been industrialised. They are forgetting that they are not producing a cider in mass for the public consumption in pubs and supermarket – those ciders have to be to suit the consumer and be consistent.

Gaymers took over Taunton cider in the late 1990s and Bob was very much involved in looking at the Taunton Cider plant. Introducing better fermentation control and yeast management was one of the investments that Mathew Clark made to improve the consistency of the brands on that site.

A word on concentrates, the percentage of fruit in cider and other hot issues

The use of concentrate is one of the major issues that has been used by the critics of large scale cider makers. I am not going to disagree. If you are claiming a heritage of Somerset cider it should be made with local apples. All through the 2000s Gaymers made a point of stating that all their own products were made with British apple juice. It was the cheaper ciders value brands etc. that tended to be made with imported concentrate. I could take you to a number of medium large cider producers where a cider apple has never crossed the threshold. I have already mentioned that there is a difference between imported general desert fruit concentrate and the concentration that a number of our leading manufacturers do with their own cider fruit to ensure all year around production.

Although not a big fan of imported concentrate Bob does have a different view to put on it than many others do. He suggests that it was the ability to use of home produced concentrated apple juice in the major brands such as Strongbow and Blackthorn in the 1970s that allowed cider to become a popular drink nationwide. Cider had always had a huge focus on the West Country. For the rest of the country supply was mainly limited to bottles – I very well remember the heavy two pint bottles with swing cap stoppers of my youth. It was concentrate that first allowed mass all year around production and the delivery of consistent keg product into pubs. It could be argued that all the success of cider over the past few decades came from the acceptance and popularity of the drink which was built on the availability of concentrate – umm – food for thought.

Because of the great British success of cider since the seventies the requirement for bittersweet apples has increased enormously. This demand has been satisfied by larger manufacturers and growers working in partnership and investing heavily in planting and orchard management. The cider industry uses over 50% of all apples grown in the UK. The major brands probably account for the use of over 80% of the bittersweet Therefore the production of concentrated English bittersweet Juice for cider making is vitally important to UK apple growing.

Bob does not like the constant references by market to the % of apple juice in the product. I confess I do – to me if you are selling it as fermented apple juice you should have that as at least the biggest proportion of the product –Bob points out that the amount and type of juice in the product is key to its character and is a key part of the recipe! Measuring content is quite complex and people have differing ideas on how to do it. What a cider tastes and looks like should be the main indicator of what it contains.

This said there is a minimum standard set regarding the amount of juice used to produce cider and perry. These are rules set by HMRC and are used for the purpose of Excise classification. In simple terms the minimum is 35% measured according to HMRC rules It is however possible to make ciders that have a projected juice content of well over 100% by using specific techniques such as adding juice for sweetening When you think about it there are a number of products like Ice cider that include more than 100% juice and a reading of the old Cider books from the seventeenth century suggest that for cider Royal and other products they were concentrating the juice. It is also obvious that with cider juice naturally fermenting out about 6% -8% ABV then the majority of commercial ciders at between 4.5% and 5.5% will have had to have been cut with water and therefore will not be 100% juice. With the government pushing for lower levels of alcohol in drinks a major challenge for the large scale cider makers is to produce weaker ciders that still taste as good as a full fruit cider. There is considerable skill to this.

None of this refutes the fact that cider in the authors view should have high apple juice content – but it does widen out the debate a bit.

Another aspect of what is a good cider that Bob wanted to discuss was to do with regional and international variation. For many people 'good' cider is the cider they are expecting and are used to drinking. We in the West Country are convinced that our cider is the best in the world. Well of course it is but we have to pay consideration to other tastes.

Bob highlights an interesting international comparison from his direct experience. 20 years or so ago he took samples of West Country cider over to a big wine-makers competition in the USA. They were convinced that the 'bittersweet' taste of the ciders was a spoilage organism and identified it with an off taste in American wines. In the past five years the cider scene in America has exploded through a 'craft' revolution – and what are they all looking for – bittersweet concentrate to make their cider. The Americans grow very few high tannin apples so they had not developed a taste for them before now.

Another example if the Australucians from Northern Spain who make occasional forays across here to promote their cider Sidra Natural. To our West Country tastes the cider is acetic in the extreme. Like many of the worst of the farmhouse scrumpys of a few years ago – and unfortunately still stumbled across all too frequently on small farm producers. These ciders are very sharp – challenging to our palates. The Australucians do have a nifty trick though – they pour into glasses from a height of over a meter – as high as they can reach in one hand and the glass as low as they can go with the other and this aerates the cider making it softer tasting. In Scandinavia, Germany and Austria they have sweet fruity drinks or apple wines that we would not label cider at all.

Perhaps the most surprising difference is that between our West Country Ciders and the ciders from the eastern counties – the partially mythical 'Eastern Style' ciders. I can remember going across to Norfolk, Suffolk and Kent 30 years ago and searching out ciders from the few small cider makers and they were thin tasting and dry and acidic in the extreme – I remember buying a pint in a pub near Dunwich in Suffolk and having to leave it – it tasted like paint stripper. The reasons for this are that they were making with culinary and desert apples and the ciders were extremely acidic with no complexity of taste. It is only in the past decade or so that reasonable 'eastern style' ciders have been produced with a whole swathe of new cider makers setting up. It has to be admitted that some of their ciders are very drinkable – if lacking in complexity. They are at their best when they retain a very fruity desert apple taste. They often rely on sweetening with pasteurised apple juice of desert varieties. However many of these 'eastern producers' make a great play that they have planted out orchards with bittersweet varieties – or even more frequently during the cider making season you see their tweets about coming to the West Country to collect apples from West Country orchards – or having lorry loads of West Country apples delivered in.

I will no doubt get stamped on by many for painting such a black and white picture and indeed it is too extreme and misleading. My son Richie will point out that a differentiation between eastern and west country ciders is identified even in the 17th and 18th century cider documents from the so called 'golden age'. Although selection of cider apple varieties was already happening at this period most cider was In fact made from whatever apples were available and many farm producers had a mixture of cider, desert and cookers in their orchards. This is very evident when you look at the heritage of ciders in counties like Dorset and Cornwall. Pomologist Liz Copas will suggest that even Somerset ciders would not have been so heavily bittersweet rooted prior to the Second World War. It was the big cider factories who planted the bittersweet orchards so they could make good cider blended with the cull desert apples they could buy cheaply from the desert fruit producing areas. One could even speculate that the presence of bittersweet apples helped disguise the blandness of cider made with imported concentrate!

Bob is keen to point out that as large scale producers they produced what the public wanted. In their range were the ciders from W Gaymer which started as far back as 1777 in the village of Banham near Attenborough in Norfolk where it survived until the 1980's. I can remember driving past the factory when visiting my maternal grandparents at nearby Hethersett. I well remember the brand Norfolk Dry – my wife Christine and I often bought in a bottle for an evening when we were first living together. And of course Christine's favourite cider has been without doubt Old English, the Gaymers cider which despite being quite sweet has an element of sharpness giving a fresh taste – the inclusion of Bramley Apples is something Bob points out when answering questions about eastern styles.

Although I may have given a black and white view, Bob with his great passion for all ciders from all points of the globe, points out that in his opinion: All Ciders are wonderful it is just that some are more wonderful than others

Anyway as we were both driving there was a definite limit to the amount we could drink and our quota ran out before the conversation. I think we are both very much looking forward to another similar 'good cider' evening in the not too distant future.

Tor Cider - 5 November

Autumn seems to be giving way ungraciously. What a wet grey, miserable day with constant drizzle interrupted by heavy outburst of penetrating wet rain. The golden hues of the very fine autumn rapidly appearing washed out as the leaves flop from the trees into the gutter. It may not yet be cold but it is still difficult to reconcile with the fact that three days ago we were in Cornwall enjoying brilliant sunshine sat outside on a pub terrace at Trebarwith Strand watching people and dogs enjoying themselves on the beach as the sun went down and the tide came in.

I have taken the opportunity of some days off work to visit a local cider maker who is in the main new to me. A year or so ago someone had given me a bottle of 'Monks Ford' from Tor Cider. I had not come across it before but was not surprised, there are a number of new cider makers springing up on the edge of the Somerset Levels encouraged by the plentiful source of apples from old orchards.

My first direct contact with them had been at the Wells Food Festival in early October when I managed to grab a couple of minutes and a few sips of tasting whilst trying to judge the trade stands. It was not a time or place for serious conversation as the huge crowds jostled to get past at what was a phenomenally successful event. We did manage to exchange business cards and James subsequently emailed and invited me over. He had read my book 'In Search of Cider' and one of the orchards he collects his apples from, just down the road from him, belongs to a couple called Pizzey and it is an orchard Richie and I had collected apples from when we first started cider making six or seven years ago.

As I pulled up James appears and I followed him through the drizzle to a nearby building. There were trays filled with pomace from previous pressings and some sacks of apples picked up that morning which they had intended to show me their pressing in action – but on such a dark wet afternoon common sense prevailed.

Under one of those marvellous pop up 3 metre by 3 metre gazebos was their Italian stainless steel mill and a pretty large hydro press – probably twice the size of ours. A bit like the mobile phone pop up gazebos have become a part of modern life which you don't know how you previously survived without. They are inexpensive and have become increasingly convenient and sturdy in providing shelter for anything from cover at a market stall, hospitality at outdoor events and of course shelter for cider making.

There are also a couple of white painted staved French grape presses – a reminder that James is also a winemaker. There is a small vineyard behind the building and he mentioned a larger one that I had spotted on the other side of the hill. They make about 3000 litres of wine and a little bit more than that of cider though it was a case of wine first followed by the cider.

This is definitely the craft end of the artisan cider spectrum – with elements of the hygiene and scientific rigour of the winemaker surpassing the enthusiasm combined with 'making do' of the majority of the artisan cider makers I know. This became very evident as I was shown the results of their previous days pressing. It had been put into a stainless steel chilling tank with bottles filled with ice dropped in to get the temperature down. Ascorbic Acid and a pectinase enzyme added and the juice was already crystal clear. We tasted a sample and it was totally clean, none of the muzzy edge that I would expect in juice pressed at this stage.

The juice was instantly recognisable from Bramley apples – not a choice of apple that is usually used for cider. But this was destined for one of their signature products. A traditional method bottle conditioned cider. We moved on into the building they use for fermentation, bottling and storage. And for producing this top end product where the winemaking knowledge certainly comes in essential.

The bottle we were to taste later was from their current batch which had been pressed in 2011. Stored for a year and a half. Bottled and kept for another year or so to allow all sediment to drop. It was then put in one of those amazing pupiter racks where it stored basically upside down and twisted regularly and the final sediment is encouraged to settle in the neck of the bottle. This neck is then frozen – they had the proper equipment for this, the top taken off and the 'plug' shoots out under the pressure that has built up. They then top up the bottle, with a small amount of sugar liquer and after further storage the cider is ready. This is field for real specialists and the master in the South West is undoubtedly Justin Mitchell of Ashridge Cider in Devon. In one of his products he adds just a touch of blackcurrant syrup at the topping up stage and produces Ashridge Blush – on of my very favourite ciders, though some purists would dismiss it as a fruit cider and therefore beyond the pale!

A look around the shed shows a predominance of stainless steel tanks – with floating lids to keep them absolutely air tight – in the sort of quantity most of us could only dream of. These are very expensive commodities. Very rare with artisan cider makers but I think most with aspirations of making good cider would love them if they could afford them – we are a long way from that! Here with 50% of the operation being dedicated to wine making they seem to be essential.

There is also a carbon dioxide injector, filling station, corkers, crown toppers, a big pasteurizer and a lot of other equipment which would make me green with envy had we somewhere to put it!

I would imagine James is in his mid-30s and makes his living from the cider and wine plus maintaining vineyards – he manages a large vineyard in Hereford and spends a couple of days a week up there. According to their business card Gill his wife is also involved in the business. James and I are joined by Steve – a long term friend and associate of his who is perhaps best described as an itinerant winemaker from Essex. Yes there is such a person. He has just come back from a spell of winemaking in France and has come down to help for a few days as he frequently does. He seems very much a part of the ethos.

We taste their four 500ml bottled ciders. These are all orchard specific and made in small batches and have a spell to condition in small wooden casks. They describe them as 'Ciders with sense of place', a phrase I like very much. These ciders matched my expectations from my fleeting tastes at the Wells Food Festival. They are quality products made to be savoured. The first noticeable feature is that they are far more vinous (wine like) than most ciders you come across. The tannins come through quite strongly though perhaps the taste is slightly more dominated by the acids than you would usually expect in Somerset bittersweet cider. This is probably adjusted in the making as the orchards they use would naturally lead to a rather low acid cider. There is also a strong influence from the casks they have been stored in. One, 'Single Barrel' has the distinctive taste of having been conditioned in a spirit barrel – but not overpoweringly so. They have all been very gently carbonated which I think is usually essential in bottled ciders. Bottling and pasteurizing without any carbonation tends to lead to a rather flat and plain taste. These four ciders are all good, clean with a depth of complex tastes – good cider.

Another feature of these ciders which I like is that they are in the main reasonably dry. Yes they use a certain amount of sweetener, they can use sugar as they are pasteurizing them, but in no case is there a 'front' taste of sweetness which blights so many modern ciders. I was also delighted to discover I could recognize a difference in taste between the ciders they matured in French oak barrels as compared to the American oak. Gosh this is sounding pretentious! But one seemed to have a more smoky taste and the other a slightly woodier aroma of logs. Perhaps I am just developing a lively imagination!

We then moved on to a bottle of the Method Champennois Bramley. This is a fine drink but perhaps not quite to my simple West Country cider taste. It is very clean and pleasant and to me tastes like a wine. However it does not have the tannins which make traditional West Country ciders so distinctive with a rich complexity of taste. It is more of clean straightforward flavour. But then again I am not a sophisticated wine taster and James and Steve admitted that part of the problem with this product is that it does not really satisfy either the cider nor the wine lover. Where to pitch it in the marketing is not a simple question. It takes a lot of effort, time and skill to make and it is a real shame that it straddles two different disciplines without really falling into one.

Just for the record we taste a bottle of 'Fine Society' our own keeved cider which I had bought along. I have got quite proficient in explaining the process of keeving these days. I am worried that this may be a bit of a sweetness shock after the dry ciders we have been drinking – but at this time of year the sweetness has in part reduced in the natural fizzing in the bottle. We have had remarkable success with this cider in the competition at the Bath and West – and in other competitions. James and Steve seem to quite like it – I don't think they were just being polite!

We get on to discussing marketing of the cider – a subject that just about all artisan cider makers wrestle with. A large part of it is examining your routes to market and developing relationships with both the public and third parties. James's main method of sales seems to be through stalls at farmers markets – and following his success at the Wells Food Festival he is looking at attending more events. He feels, quite rightly, that with a limited amount of product that maximising the margins by selling direct to the public is the most sensible way to go. Although they are a phenomena that have been growing for the last 20 years I have a slight concern that at farmers markets you are only selling to a very narrow section of the population. Over the years producers of cider and a number of other artisan food products where I have experience have suggested that the big value of farmers markets are that they creates brand awareness which leads to secondary sales. I am not convinced of this. I suspect that if people buy a bottle of good cider and like it they are more than likely to buy their next bottle in a supermarket and instead of good cider end up will less satisfactory product which just happens to be more readily available.

A question I think it is worth examining is whether the 500ml bottle is the right way of presenting a quality product. It is difficult to differentiate between your wonderful craft cider and the many hundreds of other ciders out there in 500ml bottles. Yes they are easy to sell but there is no way of getting any premium pricing – the 500ml bottle market has become commoditised whatever is in the bottle. For genuine craft makers like Tor cider should they be looking at 750ml wine bottle size? There may be problems with packaging the product to maintain the gentle carbonation which I think makes a real difference to taste – but there is much more potential to gain a pricing differentiation which the cider could well justify.

Anyway these are issues that no one will solve overnight. It has been a wonderful session and great to meet James and Steve. When cider makers get together there is always sure to be a lively and fascinating conversation. Until the next time.

It is not even four o'clock but nearly dark as I drive the seven miles back home – splashing through the puddles on the muddy slippery roads wondering why I had bothered to clean the car earlier in the week.

Wells Men's Breakfast

Jan 2016

A bit of an oddity in more ways than one this event – very much a cider event – but without drinking a drop!

I had been invited to be the speaker at the 'Wells Men's Breakfast' bright and early on a Saturday morning – getting there at 7.30 for an 8 o'clock start.

What is the Wells Men's Breakfast? I had no idea. It turned out to be in the upstairs room of a café in the centre of Wells and 60 men attend to have a cooked breakfast and a talk once a month. It has no links to any other form of organisation and does not have a membership or a subscription. There is a small organising committee and people just book themselves in – until the meeting is full. Sometimes it is oversubscribed!

As a veteran of many years of Round Table and now Rotary I am used to the formal organisation of all male organisations – but I had not come across one with quite such a loose structure as this. All the men appeared to be of a certain age – broadly speaking between 60 and 80 although there did appear to be a few like me in our 50s.

Another thing that amazed me was that in a town only 4 miles from where I live and where I work one or two days a week there were only a couple of people in the room that I had previously met plus a few familiar faces. As someone who is out and about both socially and with business this rather took me aback. It was very much a jacket and tie job and the men I spoke to seemed to be retired teachers, solicitors, engineers and others of a similar ilk. Quite a few appeared to be people who had had careers elsewhere in the country and had retired to the town.

Normally when I am at a business breakfast I am organizing them for work and I always make sure I get my breakfast last, gulp it down and then we will be ready to start the proceedings. Here I was the guest of honour and was able to get my breakfast first and eat and chat at leisure. This allowed plenty of time as with only one serving point and the need to cook extra food it took some time for all to be fed. However it was still before 9 o'clock when the chairman introduced me to do a 20 minute talk on cider in Somerset.

This was loosely the same talk and demonstration as I gave at the Somerset Food and Drink Festival in October which I have used as the opening chapter of this book. I won't go through it again but will comment that it is a lot easier to get an audience engaged in a meeting like this than standing on a stage in an exhibition. Odd problems with the microphone aside I could tell that this talk went very well – you look around at the audience and see them smiling and laughing at the right points!

One addition to my talk was the topical revision to levels of alcohol consumption recommendations which had been published by the government the previous week. Apparently it is now only safe for men to drink 15 units of alcohol in a week and this should be spread over a number of days with at least two days having no alcohol at all. Gosh this sounds alarming – I had nearly managed to restrict myself to the previous recommendation of 21 units – but to be honest that is more about monitoring my weight as a diabetic. However, many people have been raising very good questions about the validity of this new pronouncement from the Government. After all it is only about a generation or so ago when the safe limit was claimed to be eight pints a day. The reduction to 21 units, less than three units a day does not seem to have been based on any particular evidence – nor does there seem to be any sense at all to the reduction to match the recommendation of women. Yes okay we can have the jokes about women drinking – but another important consideration is weight. Are we to believe that the recommendation for a 7 stone woman is going to be the same as for a 17 stone man.

The Government recommendations go onto suggest that drinking any alcohol is not recommended and causes a greater risk of cancer. The articles I have been reading suggest very strongly that this needs to be got into perspective. Apparently the risk from drinking at the recommended level is less than watching one hour of television a day or of eating two bacon sandwiches a week! The truth is that we seem to be being dictated to by a nanny state of politically orientated neo prohibitionists. One article I read say we are being lied to. For years there have been many articles and surveys suggesting that a moderate amount of alcohol can actually reduce the risk of things like heart attack. The Government on no evidence at all are now claiming this is false. However the use of macro data allows us to see the truth. A macro data survey of over 4,000 properly conducted surveys, 88 of which are specifically on this subject from all around the world consistently shows a J shaped curve with health risk initially declining with moderate levels of alcohol consumption.

It is obvious to all that the government and their advisors are playing a political game with us moderate drinkers and the wave of reaction suggests that they have shot themselves in the foot. People are just ridiculing the announcements. There is a possible danger which that it may lead to a backlash against it – people do not like to be told to comply with false advice. I am all for moderate drinking – as an overweight diabetic I have to be. I very much warn against the dangers of binge drinking, but I want to have an objective understanding of the facts.

I managed to keep the talk down to about 25 minutes of my allotted 20! But was then asked to answer questions. At some meetings this can be an awkward spot – many people wanting to get away but a few people feeling it only polite to come up with some questions – these often ending up being about something that has already been explained or something irrelevant. Not here! The audience had obviously been listening and a forest of hands went straight up to ask excellent questions about aspects I had not had time to cover. I must have spent about ten minutes answering and there were still plenty of hands when the chairman called it to a halt – as people need to get away.

A queue of about 10 people came up to me ask further questions and I willingly spent another 20 minutes or so answering them. One question I was asked by a diabetic was extremely interesting, and to be honest I do not know the full answer. In my talk I had mentioned that a lot of the smaller artisan producers – and some bigger ones – use artificial sweeteners. Cider of course ferments down dry but the public taste is for something a bit sweeter. Unless that cider is being micro filtered or pasteurised you cannot add sugar to sweeten as it sets of the fermentation again. The largest producers will do one of the others of these processes – and incidentally strip out a lot of the complexity of flavour in the process. For smaller producers most will have their bottle product pasteurised – either in small batches themselves or by the pallet when they get it contract bottles – I am sure I will have made my thoughts known on this elsewhere. However some small producers will use artificial sweeteners instead. An a lot of the bag in box draught ciders you get in pubs will have used artificial sweetener – if you use sugar there is an embarrassing tendency for the bags to swell up – blow out the tap and deposit vast quantities of cider on the floor of the pub – not a popular selling point with landlords who you are desperate to get to stock good ciders. We can honestly say of our ciders that they contain no added sugars – and that in all but the keeved cider all the original apple sugars that were originally in there will have been fermented out.

The question is, does this make it safer for diabetics to drink? As it is nearly 20 years since I was identified as a Type II it is something that I had given some thought to in the past. And as diabetes is a progressive condition (they keep that quiet I only found our recently – I was told getting worse was down to failing to control diet!) I have had quite a lot of experience monitoring what it is that effects blood sugar levels. The generally accepted rule is that the more you eat – especially eating sweet things you sugars will go up. Controlling your diet is an essential part of control. However, there is no way that this can possibly explain the variations from day to day – week to week that I see in my blood sugars. Having a virus or cold immediately shoves blood sugars sky high – in fact it is almost an early warning system for the onset of a bug. Tiredness, stress also seem to cause blood sugars to be raised. Extra exercise does sometimes seem to bring the levels of sugars down though not on a consistent basis.

Drinking alcohol seems to have no greater effect on increasing blood sugars than any other excess in the diet. And there have been many occasions when I have got the impression that following drinking some ciders my blood sugars have been lower than I would expect. I have never followed it up but a few years ago a retired nurse who had worked all her life amongst the farming community of Somerset commented to me that drinking cider led to lower blood sugars. I have as much evidence to back this up as the Government seem to have for their alcohol consumption advice, however, I would tentatively suggest that it may be worth a bit of research to see if natural dry ciders – or natural ciders with artificial sweeteners may be an option that Type II diabetics could consider – in moderation of course.

Anyway I eventually left what I feel had been a very successful meeting. Despite living in the heart of Somerset many of those present seemed to not be aware of some of the aspects of cider and in particular the range of artisan producer's local to the area. A number of people commented to me that they were going to explore more of our local ciders. If they do that I feel that the talk was a job well done.

Wassail again, January 2016

I make no excuse for returning, a year on, to the wassail experience an important part of the finding good cider mix. Every year is different and adds to both experience and knowledge. In 2015 I went to more wassails than ever before. There was the two I am heavily involved with at North Wootton and Yarlington. In between I went to a wassail at Bere Cider down on the moors at Othery and the following Saturday I visited a new and slightly manic Wassail at the recently reopened Holman Shovel high up in the of the Blackdown Hills.

The North Wootton wassail for the Mid Somerset Show followed a very similar form to previous years. A big advance however was the saving of time in the building of the bonfire. Local solicitor Bill Bartlett made a good fist of using the tractor to help once he had managed to get out of a boggy part of the orchard where he had got stuck. The secret was discovering how to get the tractor into four wheel drive mode with the help of baker Nick Marsh – another non amateur tractor driver.

We are lucky in that Shepton Mallet logistics firm Frampton's provide us with a load of pallets most of which still have to be manhandled but this year Bill made the heart of the fire four stacks with gaps which we could roof over with other pallets. The previous year we had been trying to build a tunnel to access lighting the fire and stack pallets on top. This had collapsed a number of times and by the time it was built we were all exhausted. This year we had an equally impressive fire built in little over an hour. Yes, in rural North Wootton you can build a big bonfire on a Saturday and not have vandals light it before the Thursday of the wassail – this is a great part of the country.

I mentioned earlier in the book that at North Wootton the Wassail Princess is selected by asking the first young girl who arrives to take part. In 2016 we had a bit of a fright as it was getting quite close to the starting time before any female under 45 arrived! A young six year old girl called Issy was pounced upon as soon as she arrived. At first she looked worried but with her mum (probably the next youngest woman) in attendance she soon got into the swing of it. She scampered up ladders with confidence and enjoyed having her photo taken by the local press. When at the end she was presented with a box of chocolates for her trouble she commented that this was 'the best thing in her life!' I certainly hope there are many more good things for her.

Following my meeting with Pete Symonds in Herefordshire in the autumn I decided to add a bit of spice to my role as Master of Ceremonies by playing the role of 'The Butler'. Basically dress in a white shirt, a dinner jacket, white gloves and a black hat from a party shop. I had done some research to try to find out more about the origins of the character. Searching through books and internet searches did bring up some references. Most of these focus on mentions in Wassail Carols from the Midlands – though I believe there is also a Cornish reference from the Bodmin area. In particular one verse in the Gloucester Wassail seems to be at the root of it.

'Come Butler, come fill us a bowl of the best,

Then we hope that your soul in heaven may rest.

But is you do draw us a bowl of the small

Then down shall go Butler, bowl and all.'

From this is pretty safe to surmise that the character comes from the tradition of the 'Visiting Wassail' rather than the 'Orcharding Wassail'. More explicit speculation suggests that it was the role of The Butler to get the household together when the wassailers came to the doors and provide them with the steaming wassail bowl. The idea that the wassailers should be provided with cider fits in more with traditions like Christmas Waits and apprentices boisterously 'begging'.

I decided not to black up in the way Pete Symonds does. These days you can be pretty sure that someone would take it the wrong way. Also I could not find any reference to a tradition of The Butler blacking up. In his 'Everything you want to know about a Wassail' Pete suggests this is an element of disguise so the orchard owner would not know who it is. This once again seems to fit in more with the boisterous adventures of marauding apprentices rather than specifically with the character of The Butler. The other strand of blacking up may go back to the mummer's tradition where the person with the blacked face is associated with the devil – I am afraid I really did not want to go there in what is now basically family entertainment!

However, with my disclaimers the role seem to be well received and both wassails were successful though possibly the Yarlington one slightly less busy this year.

There were probably about 80 people there and there was a debate about whether this was due to declining popularity or whether it was the timing of 5 o'clock on a Sunday evening. I suspect a combination of these factors. It still raised over £400 for charity and given that the local pub – The Stag in Yarlington is no longer the home pub for Brue Valley Rotary I would have thought this was a good effort. They are now pondering what do next year – my suggestion would be to go to another local village to refresh it.

Between these two wassails Richie I had gone on the Saturday night to a wassail at Bere Cider at Aller on the Somerset Moors near Othery. I have written earlier as to how I think this is one of the best venues for 'finding good cider'. Jim the farmer and his wife were away on a cruise in the West Indies but his daughter and her husband Chris Smolden who makes the cider were present along with their children. Their son made an excellent job of pouring and handing out the glasses of mulled cider. Chris's wife made an excellent Wassail Queen with Chris leading the procession to carry her into the orchard. This Wassail was run by local, Gerard Tucker of the Somerton and Langport Rotary. He is also a member of Taunton Deane Morris who were the main ingredient. An enthusiastic and long established troop who mix men and women.

The ceremony was the conventional Carhampton Wassail – very close in most details to the ones I have already described. As an addition when we returned to the Cider Shed they enacted a 'Travelling Wassail' – I usually use the term 'Visiting Wassail', but they mean the same. Whilst banging on the door to get some cider bought out to us to drink to replenish the pot from the orchard we sang

For tis your wassail and tis our wassail

And it's joy be with you for tis your Wassail

One of the Morris troupe, Andrew I think, was a fellow Wassail enthusiast and had a knowledge of the Wassail Carols that far exceeded mine. He was talking about the different carols from Bodmin in Cornwall – I will have to refresh my reading.

The following Saturday was an extremely wet day but it was just damp and misty when I drove up to The Holman Shovel near Churchingford on the top of the Blackdown Hills – a wonderful remote part of the county on either side of the

A30 as Devon becomes Somerset. It is one of those pleasant remote pubs and I had been I there a number of times over the years. It had always had the air of being a bit run down and rather tatty. Since my previous visits I believe it had been shut for much of the time. However, a new dawn has risen. It has recently been taken over by Steve Watkins who for the past year has been running Tricky Cider by himself after Alistair sold out.

Steve is a smashing chap who makes some excellent traditional cider and a couple of nice bottled lines. These days he is helped on deliveries by Peter – a large gentleman past retirement who is also great fun. I had bumped into him delivering to The Sheppey a couple of weeks previously when he got a message that he had to deliver 2 boxes of cider to Nailsea the next morning. You do sometimes wonder if publicans have any idea of the cost of delivering £70 worth of cider on an 80 mile round trip!

Anyway the pub has been stripped out and now has the flagstone and pine appearance of many modern rustic pubs, appeared to have a good menu, and it was absolutely heaving with cars parked all along the road.

The wassail was being run by Dan Heath of the Cider Box, a young bearded cider wholesaler and event organiser held in great esteem in cider circles. I have a feeling that this was the first time he had run a wassail and had searched the internet to come up with every wassail idea that had ever existed and put it into the ceremony. The result was manic to the extent of almost being anarchic!

I liked the fact that a number of us were given flares to hold – these certainly added to the atmosphere even if we had trouble keeping them alight in the strong gusting wind. There must have been about 200 of us who went out on to the patio of the pub where we stood around a very young apple tree planted in a tub – a rather poor substitute for an orchard!

The ceremony started with Dan trying to get the entire crowd to walk three times around the tree in an anticlockwise direction – he sadly didn't use the wonderful word widdershins! This was an idea that had come from Steve's wife who remembered it as part of a traditional Devon wassail ceremony. Because of crowd pressure, despite a lot of jostling and shuffling I think on average the crowd only completed about two thirds of a single circuit. There was then a rather bewildering session when we 'named' the tree. The name came from the first names of the oldest and youngest person present. This took a fair bit of working out and the tree ended up with an improbable name of something like CharlottePeter. I was a bit perturbed that someone at one point wondered if I was the oldest – at 58 do I look that bad? Richie would say yes!

At least the Wassail Princess had been preselected. A number of years ago I went to a Wassail at Somerset Rural Life Museum where the ceremony was held up while we all had a bit of apple cake one piece of which had a bean in it and the person who got the bean became Wassail Queen or King. Still this ceremony seemed to be taking long enough. The usual constituents took place now – though putting the toast in the branches and pouring cider round the roots was a bit tame with the sapling in a pot.

We then moved on to the climax with the singing of the Wassail Carol. I had heard the folk musicians warming up okay and heard the safe tune of 'Miller of Dee' for the standard Carhampton Carol. In this instance rather than going straight through the carol we seemed to go back and repeat the middle part of the carol twice when we should already have been doing the shouted response section about Hat Fulls and Capfulls. This only arrived after we had sung the carol through twice and only then as a separate item!

For safety reasons the chap with the shotgun had retreated behind the buildings off the patio. He shot three times and I think most of the crowd may have caught one of them about the general noise level.

All in all it was great fun and certainly different. As I have said before there is no right and wrong with a wassail – it is all about engagement and enjoyment and we were all certainly doing that. I retired into the pub to quaff another pint of Steve's rather good Tricky dry cider and sat talking to some very interesting likeminded people before setting off through the dark and mist and puddles on the long drive home.

Dan Heath – CiderBox

A few weeks after the Holman Clavell Wassail I arranged to meet Dan in a pub to find out more about him and what he does. We had known each other for a couple of years but have never had long enough for a sensible meeting. We met in the Cross Keys at Lydford – now an excellent pub with a reasonable choice of Ciders. I went with the excellent Harry's Cider from nearby Long Sutton. Tom the manager although still young has run some excellent pubs. On a previous visit he had started to talk to me about the possibility of him doing a cider festival in September – could be exciting.

Dan – is the CiderBox. He is young, articulate and passionate about spreading the word of good cider. I asked Dan about the origins of his business. 'It started by accident' was the simple explanation.

Dan, a fellow real ale and cider fan from the West Country, had migrated to London for a 10 year stretch. Talking to a publican he discovered they could not get hold of Somerset Artisan ciders. So, as you do, he volunteered to bring a box back next time he visited Somerset. Once he had done it once he found himself doing it more and more.

He then started doing events in pubs and elsewhere where he started the process of explaining what Somerset cider is about. He quickly became a practiced and popular speaker on the subject. Those who have heard him giving his tutored tastings at the Bath and West certainly speak highly of him. He started moving more and more cider back to London provisioning a growing variety of outlets. After a few years it built to a significant business – though only really became full time in 2015.

Dan has a philosophy that the cider he promotes really should be the proper stuff and he is willing to tell people what that is and isn't. He is now talking to some of the smaller pub chains in London and working with them not only on their cider stocking but also on getting them to work with some of the key West Country artisan producers to produce own brand ciders. The running of traditional cider through pub coolers to produce a slightly fizzy cider is one of the areas that is developing rapidly at the moment as smaller cider producers come to terms with providing what the pubs and the public want. He is currently negotiating to supply a chain of 60 London pubs – an exciting opportunity.

Before last Christmas Dan ran a Christmas market near Temple Meads station in Bristol. Although not a failure he discovered that the location was not ideal as the footfall was mainly in the very short period when people were on their way home from work. However, I am sure Dan will come up with further ideas to experiment with. He seems to have the right blend of loyalty to the tradition, entrepreneurship and innovation to make things happen.

Currently he is a one man wholesaler based out of his van. Talking to Dan I discovered that his limited van space combined with the weight of cider has led to him getting stuck at a couple of cider producers. At Mark Venton's his van would not make it up the drive – especially when he went off the concrete trackway. I do rather sympathise here as I usually park outside on the road – the driveway is particularly steep and on a sharp curve. However, Dan also related that the previous week he had managed to wreck Neil Worley's lawn. Yes the ground is extremely muddy at the moment and the track besides Neil's is sometimes like a running stream but this is somewhere I have been many times and had never felt the urge to go on the lawn. It reminds me of Mad Apple Cider – a Somerset cider maker from the Quantocks. When picking up apples from local orchards he would drive in with his pickup firmly in four wheel drive mode with locked wheels. He still needed to carry with him a winch which he could wrap around trees to lever himself out when he got stuck. There is something about cider that seems to lead to a lot of us overloading our vehicles for one reason or another.

The next thing I want to happen is for Dan to start sourcing some of his cider from Stone's Bittersweet!

The Closing of the Shepton Cider Mill

On the 12th of January 2016 C&C brands – owners of both Magners Cider and the Shepton Cider Mill announced that they were are going to close the Shepton Cider Mill in about July 2016 with the loss of around 120 jobs with production being transferred to Clomell in Ireland.

After a couple of days it became clear that as they have a lot of contracts with orchards in the West Country they would be keeping an element open to mill the apples and concentrate the juice before transporting the juice to Ireland. Four people would retain their jobs and more would be seasonally employed. Somehow this does not seem an arrangement that has an air of permanency around it.

C&C brands made a big hash of releasing the news. Apparently the story was leaked in the Irish Trade Press in the morning and it was very quickly picked up by the British press. I had Mendip District Council on the phone by 10 o'clock to see if I could help them with some contact details. By 11 o'clock the Mid Somerset Series of Newspapers (Shepton Mallet Journal) had been on wanting my reaction and by 12 o'clock BBC Somerset had contacted me wanting me to do a live interview on the radio the following morning – I was rather surprised and flattered that so many saw me as a key contact! A few days later I was also interviewed for regional television news on the state of Somerset cider – filmed at the excellent Sheppey at Godney along with landlord Mark Hey!

By midday the press had got a reaction out of C&C brands if only to say there would be a statement that afternoon but not denying the truth of the story. The statement confirming the story came that afternoon. The really annoying thing is that the story was already well out there before the staff were informed.

Although the media made a big thing out of the element of surprise around the closure the truth is that it did not come as a surprise, except maybe in exact timing, to anyone who knew anything about the plant and the ongoing run down since C&C Brands bought it in 2009. C&C claimed at the time, and have reiterated since, that they bought it to grow the business and had made major investment. It did not turn out like that.. C&C brands was at that time still riding high on the big expansion of Magners in the previous five years as the 'cider over ice' fad swept the country. However, this had started to run out of steam and was not making the progress that was wanted particularly in the South and West of the country. They saw Shepton Cider Mill as an opportunity to buy some market share and switch more business into Magners.

As far as I am aware they never switched any production of Magners into Shepton Mallet. Magners was made in Ireland. However, after a six month delay waiting for approval of the deal, they moved firmly to try to switch existing Shepton Mallet brands into Magners which became their 'pole' product. The marketing lady at Shepton Mallet was made redundant – ending local support and marketing for the brands. I was told at the time that the national marketing budget for Blackthorn, which then was either the second or third biggest brand in the country was chopped to 30% of its previous level. All of the sports sponsorships etc ended as soon as they could manage it. The popular Gaymers Cider – which had been a big success over the previous three years was just axed. It was thought to be too similar a cider to Magners. The brand limped on with some fruit ciders for the younger market.

Marketing support for the other brands such as Olde English, K, Natch seemed to wither and it rapidly became increasingly hard to even get hold of them. But the vacuum in the market place was not switched to Magners. The biggest beneficiary was Thatchers who because of their blackcurrant crushing contract for Ribena had one of the most modern cider mills in Europe and a cider heritage story which was very appealing in the West Country. It was also a period where there was a diversification in the market place – smaller producers got a bigger toe in some doors and the alchopop market turned its attention to fruit ciders. Then the big lager brewers seeing cider as a potential new market started getting their ciders produced for them and further distorted the cider market place.

In defence of C&C a fact that has been conveniently forgotten was that their purchase of the Shepton Cider Mill was a distress purchase at a very low price. Previous owners Constellation Europe wanted out and did not see it as part of their future. The mill had changed hands a few times over the previous 20 years and the brands were already struggling to keep their place in the dynamic cider market. However, C&C Brands effectively appeared to stymie all the Shepton brands to a position from which they could not recover. The closure of the Shepton Mill had become an inevitability.

Things were beginning to go wrong for C&C brands. Growth in the overall cider market slowed and with increased production capability margins began to be squeezed. Once they realised it was not going to be a case of Magners just gaining market share they made some attempts to revive the Shepton brands. They set up a new marketing team to promote them. Sadly, this team seemed to lack the resource to revive old brands or establish new. Time moves on and trying to revive brands you have just run down is not likely to be successful and they were given little time.

C&C invested in a new bottling line – but without volume to bottle this was mothballed from its inception and by all accounts is now only raided as spares. They did go out and try to gain some of the contracts that were available in the market place. It is an open secret that the Belgium cider 'Stella Cidre – 'not cider but cidre,' one of the more successful lager brand ciders was made and packaged in Shepton Mallet. I asked which part of Belgium Shepton Mallet was in and was told 'Belgium Style'.

Not quite so well-known is the fact that Thatcher's Gold in its bright yellow cans was canned in Shepton Mallet – this was probably the biggest element of work keeping the factory open in 2015. Good stuff, I drink many cans of it, but the point is that the margins on this sort of contract work are narrow did not make a sustainable basis for the factory.

Credit to C&C – they did try to invent some new products. As already mentioned including the excellent Chaplin and Cork. They appointed as director of the Shepton Cider Mill an Italian called Paulo. He made serious efforts to re-engage the cider mill with the local community and come up with ideas that would re-invigorate the mill. He resigned in late 2014 and in the spring of 2015 – he had not had enough time to focus on achieving the turn around. It became clear that no direct replacement had been appointed. Many people would probably be correct in assuming that C&C brands had by then made up their minds.

For the work force the decline had been nearly relentless. By the time of the closure most of the old hands with expertise and experience had gone. I have spoken to former factory staff, proud of the job they had done, who related a tale of practically being forced into early retirement. The plant had no local management but was being run from Glasgow and foremen were sent down who were described to me as 'little more than bullies'.

The announcement is really sad for those 120 remaining. Some with over 30 years' experience – what does the future hold for them. The workforce at Shepton Cider Mill have been their best ambassadors. They have been justly proud of their products. I talked to one worker who was responsible for calibrating the plant to be able to make Stella Cidre. They talked about the fine tuning it took to get a consistent product with exactly the right profile. There was a new products last year – a stronger version of Olde English, Olde English 1777. The staff were really pleased with it and it was a best seller in the staff shop – but you never ever saw it anywhere else and it was quickly withdrawn. In no way can the workforce be held in any way to blame for the short coming of the management and marketing acumen of the parent company.

If there is any silver lining it is that one suspects the local job market will soak them up pretty quickly. There is a lot of food and drink businesses within Shepton Mallet and within the central Somerset area in general. There is a real need for engineers, fork-lift drivers and the like. There is a general shortage of labour. The media talking about the disaster it will have on the local economy are probably exaggerating. However this does not make it better for the individuals – they will have been hurt.

The town of Shepton Mallet will have been hurt as well. It will have suffered a major blow to its already very low self-esteem. Quite why Sheptonians have such a low opinion of their own town is a constant mystery but in the local history studies I have made it appears to be an attitude that is nearly 100 years old. They were already holding 'Shop in Shepton' weeks to try to boost local retail in the 1930s!

In fact Shepton has a surprisingly strong economy. It is a net importer of labour, there are more jobs than potential workers, and a thing that surprises many is that it has a bigger retail area than any of the other Mendip Towns with the exception of Street where they have of Clarkes Village.

It is a real blow to the drink manufacturing heritage of the town. Shepton Mallet was famed for Babycham and the cider followed on from that. Having the second biggest cider mill in the world was something to be proud of. However closer examination of the history does not fully substantiate the view that Shepton was the centre of the cider world. The press picked up on the fact that cider had been made in Shepton since the mill was founded in 1770. They are in fact referring to W Gaymers who as already mentioned made cider in Norfolk and the subsequent company only moved fully to Shepton in the 1990s.

One suspect's cider was made in Shepton for longer than that and I believe the Showering family were publicans and brewers in the town going back to the 1650s – they probably made cider all that time too. They are supposed to have bought the brewery on the site that they later grew from in the 1850s. By the 1930s when it was run by the four Showering Brothers it was a growing business and Babycham put it on the national map in the 1950s.

Babycham excepted the real growth in cider production came as recently as the 1960s and 70s when it was part of Allied Breweries. They had an acquisition policy. Whiteways – a national cider brand from Devon was bought, Coates from Nailsea in Somerset, Gaymers from Norfolk and finally Blackthorn from Taunton. In every instance they kept the mill in the home town open for a period and then transferred production to Shepton Mallet. Each of those towns has gone through the pain of having their cider mill closed. In a supreme piece of irony the Magners Mill in Clomell in Ireland was at one time Showerings Ireland. It is the only place in the world other than Shepton Mallet where Babycham had been made!

To an extent, despite feeling desperately sorry for the workers, one has to be a bit philosophical about the closure. Shepton Mallet as a town will go on. There is still very much a cider heritage in the town with the thriving Brothers Drinks / Mallets Cider run by the next generation of Showerings. There are new producers in and near the town like Pilton Cider, Worley's and even our own Stones Bittersweet. There are other makers and more will follow. I suspect that at some time the town will find a way of linking it cider heritage to tourism. Life will go on and it is still to be hoped that some phoenix may rise from the ashes of the cider mill.

In the proof stages of this book there is some sign of a sort of Phoenix. The Showering brothers of Brothers Drinks have bought the buildings on the east side of the A37 and the multimillion pound unused bottling line. This will be added to their existing two bottling lines in The Anglo Trading Estate on the other side of town to boost their capacity. It is unclear how many jobs this will save. Brothers say they will be looking for engineers but other than that it may be the limited amount of labour needed comes mainly from their existing workforce of 120 in the town. It will take them time to find the extra work needed to utilise the capacity, In the same week in early April it has been announced that they have made the last batches of Blackthorn, Natch, Addlestones and Olde English in Shepton before production is transferred to Ireland. C&C and the Unite Union are still talking about finding a seller though as they are not willing to sell the brands the purpose is removed – the latest rumour is that it could become a canning plant for the beer a national brewery.

Devon – Cider Tourism

February 2016

I thought I would have a day being a cider tourist. Part of the reason for this was that I had a feeling that to get a sense of balance in this book I needed a greater focus on Devon. Trips to the far side of Exeter – or out into the Devon countryside are relatively rare for me – so making the effort to go tends to suggest I am being a tourist – and cider tourism is a topic I should be covering anyway.

In some ways I am the ultimate cider tourist – well excluding the international cider tourists like Bill Bradshaw and Pete Brown for their book the World's Greatest Ciders. It is a very interesting book but personally I have found the majority of International ciders I have tried rather disappointing compared to our West Country ciders. I have met, visited and sampled at least 150 cider makers over the past decade – quite probably over 200 but I would need to have a count up. I accept this would probably not be seen as normal behaviour but there are quite a number of people who just like visiting different cider makers. Usually this requires an element of cider tasting but it is not just that which drives people on. I feel it is part of the 'good cider' experience. Encompassing product, heritage and the social aspects, exploring some of the most beautiful and deserted parts of the West Country it is very a very worthwhile activity. I admit to a sense of pride the first time I was on an artisan cider makers and I saw a visitor holding one of my books which was clearly guiding him around. It is nice to think I am helping people discover some of our artisan producers.

On the whole cider tourism is an independent activity. I have been amazed at the number of retired couples I come across who list a considerable number of cider farms as places they have visited. Maybe I shouldn't be amazed, I was talking to a diversified farmer who has opened a coffee shop in his farm buildings – mainly to capitalise on the staff of the number of businesses who operate from his converted farm buildings. Much to his surprise, especially given the obscure location, most of his visitors are people who go out and explore different coffee shops. There is a sort of a circuit for groups the early retired, often women, and their friends.. Some cider makers seem to combine the two things and a good number of cider makers have a coffee shop or tea room as part of their attraction.

Talking of which quite a number of cider producers do set themselves out to be a bit of a tourist attraction. Healy's Cornish Cider Farm is the champion which a claimed 400,000 visitors a year! But there are many others around the country. In Somerset we have the likes of Perry's, Sheppy's and Rich's who have a small heritage display, cider sales and tea rooms combined. There are others around the country.

Another element of Cider tourism is the organised visits and tours. Evenings where local organisations come in to see the cider farm and have bread cheese and plenty of cider are popular with groups from Young Farmers to Rotary with only the element of drinking varied! In Somerset Roger Wilkins of Mudgely near Wedmore is the master of this -£10 a head for plenty of bread, cheese and all you can drink!

In recent years it has been interesting to see some tours of different producers being organised. In the usual format a minibus full of people come down the M5 either from London or the Midlands. They have the advantage of having a driver so people are free to drink. There are a number of producers within easy reach of the M5. Crossman's at Congresbury, John Harris, Westcorft at Brent Knoll, Richs at Highfield, Sheppy's at Bradford on Tone to name only a few. They can then come on down to try some of the Devon producers before wending their way back home.

Today I was trying to do a bit of the Devon end and catch up with three producers who had I felt guilty at not making the effort to visit during the previous year – though all of whom I had visited before.

Sam's Cider – produced by Winkleigh Cider Company

I decided to start at the further end of my day's itinerary by visiting Winkleigh Cider which I had visited four years before when researching In Search of Cider and met the owner David Bridgman. Earlier in the book you may remember I had met his daughter and son in law Kylie and Chris Beardon at The Source, Taste of the West Trade Show who are now running the business – though David is still involved. David's son James is also working there and learning the art of cider making. Kylie and Chris had struck me with their enthusiasm – it is obvious they are breathing exciting new life into a fairly traditional business. Everything I have seen since and saw on this visit reinforces that impression.

New brand, new equipment and buildings and a new focus on an element of innovation into their cider.

The journey to Winkleigh was a delightful drive on a cold and frosty morning. This part of West Devon always surprises me. It is a vast area of pasture and arable farming land where the many farms are just about the only habitations in the rolling rural landscape. I know the A30 very well as it has made the trip down to Cornwall so easy. In fact for a time I commuted three days a week from Shepton Mallet to Lifton which is just before you reach the Cornish border. However, if you turn right off the A30 there is a huge mass of farmland stretching the considerable distance to the North Devon Coast about which I know very little and am amazed by whenever I venture out into it. It is a succession of rolling landscape and valleys. One thing you soon discover is that if you are heading cross-country rather than back into Exeter the roads never seem to head in the direction you expect them to. The journey from the A30 to Winkleigh is all actually on pretty major roads but the number of junctions and turnings was far from intuitive. If it was not for diligent attention to the signposts I think you would be unlikely make it without getting lost.

You could see Winkliegh on the side of its hill from about two valleys away and the Cider Factory is very easy to find on the eest of the village.

2016 sees their 'Centenary'. Well it is the centenary of when the legendary Sam Inch first made cider as a youth during the Great War when he was given some apples in lieu of wages for doing some work so the legend goes. Sam carried on making a bit of cider alongside his other work for the period between the wars. Most cider making was at that time small scale but after the war Sam started to bottle his cider and expand the business. It grew significantly and by the 1960s quite a factory had developed and Inch's Cider was one of the better known names. Apparently the factory was employing over 90 people including from 1966 the young David Bridgman who has been there ever since. Eight artic loads of cider were leaving the site every day in its prime.

After Sam Inch died in1986 his son took over but did not have the same enthusiasm. Three years later he sold out to an ambitious partnership. Despite earlier assurances, the factory was shut. Reluctantly they allowed David to buy only a part of the once large business and to carry on some small scale cider making. They were determined it would not compete with them and smashed all but four of the large wooden 10,000 gallon vats. The four are only smaller versions of what Inch's used to have. Inch's had 16,000, 20,000 and even as big as 40,000 gallon oak vats! David was not allowed to use the name 'Inch's' so it became branded as 'Sam's' cider and has carried on for the past 20 years.

But now it is moving forward apace. It had been a big decision for Chris and Kylie to take on the business, they both had to give up their previous jobs. Kylie was a veterinary nurse whilst Chris had been a steel fabricator, welding stainless steel, definitely a useful experience to have. However, they now seem really up for the challenge – along with raising their two young children, and with another arriving in the height of the busy season this year. Chris is definitely interested in ensuring their cider is the best they can produce. One of its characteristic features is a very pale straw colour and perhaps giving the perception of being a bit light – a bit like the very sinkable ciders made by the Rich's in Somerset. I suspect this mainly comes from the varieties of apple they use but Chris is exploring as to whether there is anything in the way they make the cider or the timing of pressing that may be affecting it. To me their cider is already tasting a degree of so better than some I have had in the past – though that may be in my imagination. There is also a new cider, crafted for the 'centenary'. This is a more rich and complex cider with a deeper colour and more complex taste. He suggested it is a bit on the sweet side but to me it was only as sweet as many of the mediums that are marketed these days.

The site and equipment is undergoing a transformation as well. They do all their bottling themselves on a small 2 head bottler. Last year they invested in some new labelling equipment. This year they are having a new bottling line built for them by Vigo. To accommodate this they are demolishing some of the old post-war concrete buildings which are not only unattractive but impractical and they have plans to put up a new packing and distribution shed. This will be an ongoing process as they seek to maximise the potential of their site. Already 25% of their total turnover comes from trade through their on-site shop which is open 6 days a week all year around. Given its rather remote setting, far from the beaten track is is surprising how busy it gets, particularly in the summer tourist season and then there is the rush just before Christmas.

Kylie has plans to develop the visitor experience with a small heritage centre. They would like to open it up so that visitors can see their four amazing surviving timber vats. There is also of course scope for reviving a tea room as they move on and increase footfall. Chris had just returned from a trip to Holland with a number of leads he is following up to increase their fledgling export trade. There is a lot going on and I certainly wish them all the best. This is one for the cider tourist and more than that one for disciples of the concept of 'good cider'!

Sandford Orchards Cider

I made my way 15 miles back to Crediton, near neighbours in this sparsely populated landscape! One of West Country ciders rising stars and certainly a true character had invited me a year ago to come and see his new premises and this was the first chance I have had. About eight years ago when I first met Barney Butterworth of Sandford Orchards Cider he was still a small producer who had just taken on the tenancy of a farm down a long track just outside Crediton. I visited there a number of times – and even on occasion managed to catch him! He is an energetic chap who is here, there and everywhere. His business quickly started to grow and he invested a lot of time into it and was not adverse to financial gambles!

Over the years I have met him at many exhibitions and show. He is this year's Chairman of SWECA the South West Cidermakers Association of which I am a small producer member. Early in 2015 he managed to purchase a large factory building on the eastern edge of a Crediton trading estate. It may not be the most romantic of settings but if you are looking for cider heritage it has this in bundles.

In the 20th century and before Crediton had a big tradition as a cider making town. Sadly with business takeovers and natural wastage it had declined and for the past 40 or so years as with so many towns the heritage was just a memory. The huge building Barney has bought was the home of Creedy Valley Cider who were one of the major cider producers in Devon – probably more in the interwar years and predating Inch's at Winkleigh. Barny speculates that some of the equipment from Creedy Valley went to Winkleigh as they expanded in the 1950s.

Barney has moved most of his production and storage to the factory – though he has retained some of his operation on the farm. Unlike many less scrupulous he feels that the appellation of 'farmhouse cider' does mean it has to come from a farm – particularly when dealing with the likes of M&S. Between the two sites he now has storage for 1.2 million litres of cider – a rapid growth over the past eight years.

Partly because of his rapid growth Barney has faced accusations that he is now an industrial cider maker with all the negative connotations that that implies. I have argued with people on the internet about this – as far as I can see it is not justified. Barney's cider is made in a traditional way from the fresh pressed juice of cider apples fermented at ambient temperature – which in the factory today was rather on the chilly side! He is making in the same way as all artisan or craft cider makers but on a bigger scale. His 10 tonne per hour belt press is more than impressive. A massive beast which dwarfs the 3 tonne and hour belt press on which Neil Macdonald crushes our apples or the press at Winkleigh Cider I had seen only an hour earlier but works in exactly the same way with the same results. His apples come from traditional local Devon orchards and he has planted extensively himself.

I think others misunderstood Barney because of what I admit is his wide rather bewildering range – with different and often unrelated names for the different Ciders. Like the cider I try on this visit – Old Kirton – or another called Shaky Bridge. Yes there are good stories and reasons behind the names but for the punter simple 'still' or 'sparkling' and 'sweet' 'medium' or 'dry' would be more helpful to identify what you are looking for. He also was one of the faster people to try a fruit cider with 'Fanny Bramble'. It is a big market and smaller producers have to respond. The duty regulations ensure that this can only be 4% alcohol so of course a certain amount of water has to be added to reduce the strength, but this does not affect the integrity of the bulk of his ciders!

The western end of the factory has the offices and a large area has been converted to an attractive cider bar with tables and off sales. It is open six days a week and provides an ideal setting for the cider tourist to visit either to buy a drink or off sales. He is developing it as a bit of a venue. That evening there was an event for his 'Secret Cider Drinkers Club.' Each month they get a local food business with a 'pop up' kitchen to come in and prepare a four course meal which they then match with the right ciders to drink – usually including a guest cider from another manufacturer. These can only hold up to 40 people and are usually sold out. I understand that Curries were the subject for that evening's meal – which seems a sound idea as they would certainly need something to heat them up!

Barney is a great believer in cider heritage. He has bought an old Creedy Valley Cider delivery lorry – for more than he should have spent. But the story I liked most was about the cooperage tools that he has on display. These belonged to the last cooper in the factory, Owen Burrage, who had made the last barrel in about 1965. Barney knew him as a rugby coach when he was playing during his youth. When Barney moved into the factory last year the elderly Owen said he wished he had known that Barney was bringing cider making back to Crediton. He had tried to get local museums to take his old tools but no one appeared interested. In the end Tuckers Maltings, a historic maltings near Topsham had taken them and put them on display. Barney phoned them up and explained the connection with his factory and asked if there was any chance he could buy them.

Just about the next day the tools were delivered to the factory. He phoned up to ask what they would cost him and was told that there was no charge. The directors had had a chat and they strongly felt that the tools should be at the Crediton factory. It is the sort of story that brings tears to my eyes even as I type it. Sometimes this is a wonderful country with some wonderful people who really have a strong sense of our heritage.

Barny and his ciders deserve to be on any tour for those 'finding good ciders'.

Venton's Devon Cyder

From Sandford Orchards I drove through Exeter and out into the lanes the other side in my attempt to find the tiny East Devon village of Clyst St Lawrence – which believe it or not currently has three different cider makers, Venton's, Crafty and Berry Farm. All of which definitely make 'good cider'. David Rowe makes for the last two mentioned but I was here to catch up with Mark Venton.

The problem with Clyst St Lawrence is that whatever direction you come from it is almost impossible to find. I think I had been here five times and still checked the map beforehand and both coming and going I am sure I took a long route. I came via the old A30 at Whimple. Well it is not the A30 anymore, that takes a new route but the old road is being converted into a series of roundabouts leading to half built housing estates as Exeter builds a massive extension to its east. Anyway I follow what I think is the route and after what seems like 5 miles I come across a sign pointing down a different lane saying Whimple 2 miles. The same happened on the way back although I was taking a totally different route. On my first visit to the village I had printed off a google map – only to discover that the postcode covered more than one farm a good couple of miles apart – Devon!

Mark Venton is a great chap. He was, and still is to a lesser extent, a builder and site manager. He had started making cider (or cyder as he prefers) when he moved into his cottage and saw all the apples left around going to rot. He built a traditional screw press out of oak and with his wife Sharon, sons, neighbours and friends he started making cider. He had an early success at the Devon County Show and has taken it from there.

He is very much a traditional producer. Even this winter when he produced 27,000 litres in the hope that he can eventually become a full time cyder maker, none of the cider apples came from any further away than four and a half miles. He still presses a lot of his cider through clean straw which has become his trademark. However, building traditional cheeses and pressing them out cannot be rushed and limits output so he also now uses a small hydraulic pack press as well.

It is all produced in his 'shed'. Admittedly it is a fair sized shed and it has had an extension added all along one side since I was last here, but it is still absolutely crammed full and negotiated with care! He started fermenting in old oak barrels and is still using these for maturing his ciders. However, most of the fermentation now take place in huge 1,500 litre juice tanks. In the shed known as 'The Cyder Barn' he does all the blending, bottling, experiments and much more!

Mark is a serious thinker about cider and what he does. Although very much a traditionalist he makes sure he understands the whole science. This is why his ciders always taste clean and good. Readers of my previous books will know that my experience of traditional ciders, pressed through straw and stored in oak has far from always been good. I think in my very first book I identified that a few of the best ciders I tasted on my travels fitted this description – so also did all of the worst! Mark is not adverse to progress. The first stainless steel tank with a sinking lid has appeared and he had a very nice digital flow meter for filling bag in boxes which may be the next thing we invest in at home.

Fortunately Mark is very much in the area of the best ciders. I went in for a quick catch up and of course ended up staying for over three hours. During that time we had caught up on each other's cider gossip, put the world to rights on many cider issues and sampled his current stock dry cider and did the 'Tour of the Barrels' around at least eight of his tanks pressed in the autumn to see how they were progressing. The answer was very well indeed.

It will not have escaped anyone's attention that my cider tastes have evolved to a love of good dry ciders where the taste of the apples and orchard comes through. My favourite cider of the time researching this book is probably the ciders of Mike Johnson of Ross on Wye cider, but these ciders run it very close. 'good cider' or in this case 'cyder' – what better way is there of spending an afternoon talking about cider and sampling it in a genuine cider shed!

As always when artisan cider makers get together one of the topics of conversation was where you sell your cider. Producing it is hard work but really the enjoyable part of it. Selling it is the hard grind – especially when like Mark you are increasing sales and trying to make a living out of it. He sells a lot through festivals and events all over the country and is increasing the number of events he and Sharon attend themselves such as the Devon County Show. Quite a bit of his cider goes through a few Cider wholesalers who specialise in supplying cider festivals. To my surprise Mark doesn't major on selling to free house pubs and named only a handful in Devon. He says the demand for draught cider is very seasonal and reliant on holidaymakers in rural pubs but some are supportive all year round. The Tom Cobley which I had passed on my way to Winkleigh that morning, The Warren Inn at Postbridge, an excellent pub with a landlord who has been there for years way up on Dartmoor, The Pony and Trap in Cullompton and The Old Fire House in central Exeter which is another excellent pub which I always contrive to visit when I am in the city. It could be the natural reserve with which a cider maker protects his outlets but I am sure there must be more than that.

For me this is the ultimate in cider tourism. However Mark does not have an off sales licence. Like us he can only sell to wholesalers. Some of the minibus tours come here by prearrangement to find this cider mecca but it is not open to the general public – and I think the shed would need a good tidy before it could be! Mark would love in a year or two to get an off sales licence but feels it would be very hard to obtain and could open up a big can of worms in the village. However, if you are a true disciple of cider please do give him a ring and see if you can arrange a visit it is certainly worth the experience. Check him out on Facebook Ventons Devon Cyder – or ring him on 07811 963853

Devon could make a lot more of its cider tourism potential. Both Somerset and Hereford have produced cider trail leaflets which are widely available. There would seem to be a crying need for something similar in Devon. There may not quite be as many different makers as in Somerset but in terms of numbers of producers it is certainly the second most important cider making county.

Finding Good Cider in the age of the Scientific Revolution

Dr R G Stone

Finding good cider. This is a quest with a surprisingly long history, and one which considerably predates the modern 'foodie' revolution. Indeed, it even predates the old chestnut of a story about itinerant farmhands going from one farm to another at harvest time until they found the place with the best cider. It is, in fact, a story which we can trace all the way back to Tudor England, with the unlikely figure of Henry VIII as one of its pioneers. When Henry wasn't otherwise engaged asset stripping the monasteries or adding to his collection of wives, he found the time to encourage his head gardener, Richard Harris, to plant orchards all over the south of England. In later centuries, many writers were to see this as the foundation stone of England's love affair with the apple, and with the drink which it yielded.

My focus in this chapter, though, is on another group of cider enthusiasts, although in many ways an equally surprising one. This is the members of the nascent Royal Society, some of England's finest minds in the decades after the Civil War, and the vanguard of the Scientific Revolution. At much the same time as they were discussing new ideas such as the circulation of blood, or advanced optics, these men dedicated a considerable portion of their time and energy to seeking out ways to make the best cider. Many papers were delivered to the Society by a diverse range of contributors, and indeed one of their very first publications included *Pomona, or an Appendix Concerning Fruit-Trees In relation to Cider* edited by the well-known diarist John Evelyn. Its authors included men from a wide range of backgrounds, such as the Herefordshire (and later Somerset) clergyman Dr. John Beal; Yorkshire landowner Sir Paul Neil; Parliamentarian army officer Captain Sylas Taylor; and London merchant and philanthropist Daniel Colwall.

That such a prestigious and intellectual group of men should be so interested in cider is perhaps not as surprising as it might at first sound. The Royal Society was very much focused on *useful* enquiry, finding out about things which would be of benefit to the nation as a whole. In this regard, cider fitted the bill perfectly! In his introduction to *Pomona*, John Evelyn clearly set out his reasons for promoting cider. It was, he said, 'one of the Mos[t] delicious and wholesome beverages in the world'. Well of course, it doesn't take a great scientific mind to work that one out! Evelyn naturally, though, sought to prove this with the most rigorous of scientific methods by getting an unsuspecting London public to compare cider to wine in blind taste tests. Unsurprisingly, they chose the cider as their favourite every time (although one does wonder if they may have been nudged in the right direction...).

Evelyn also argued that cider can 'soberly exhilarate the spirits of us Hypochondriacal Islanders'. I'm absolutely fascinated by this... Discussions of the health benefits of drinking cider have been about for a long time, but I've not heard many people claim that it makes you 'sober'! Perhaps this had something to do with the strong association between cider, orchards, and nature. Continuing his case for cider, Evelyn wrote that 'the very blossom of the fruit perfumes, and purifies the Ambient Air, which... conduces so much to the constant Health and Longevity'. Clearly, he argued, if the people of England drunk more cider, they would be much healthier and longer lived. Writing at the time of a Junior Doctors strike, I can't help wondering whether this might be a sensible policy for the government to adopt today in order to solve the NHS budgetary crisis...

Another author, the clergyman and horticulturalist Ralph Austen, took this argument a step further in his 1653 work *The Spiritual Use of an Orchard*. For him, the increased consumption of cider and resultant propagation of fruit trees was not just good for the body, it also benefitted the spirit. Austen was part of a broader trend of interest in the natural world which was developing in the seventeenth century, seeking by understanding of it to gain a greater knowlege of the nature of God. God, after all, had created the world, therefore he had created the orchard, and therefore he had created cider. By understanding these things more fully you would thus understand Him (the Creator, and therefore ultimately the cider maker?) better. For Austen, by drinking cider or even simply being in an orchard, you came closer to God. Indeed, so convinced was he of this belief, as well as of the other benefits of orcharding, that Austen even petitioned Parliament to insist that apple trees must be planted on every acre of newly enclosed land.

Other arguments for the promotion of cider in the mid-seventeenth century were much more mundane. Drinking cider, Evelyn argued, would benefit the nation in economic terms. The arguments for this were twofold, comparing cider favourably to both beer and wine. At a time known by climate historians as

'The Little Ice Age' (with the Thames repeatedly freezing over during the long cold seventeenth century winters) cultivation of grapes in England was no easy task. For wine, therefore, Englishmen had to turn to the warmer climes of France and Spain. This was a long time before the European Union, and a sophisticated understanding of the international economy. For Evelyn and his contemporaries, therefore, to buy wine from a foreign country was simply to pour gold into the hands of England's economic rivals. Why do this when England's own soil could yield an even finer drink? And one, furthermore, which would still be available even during the numerous wars and trade embargoes which characterised the era, and cut England's merchants off from their yearly booze cruise to France and Spain.

Drinking beer too, was economically bad sense (not to mention that, rather than extending your lifespan (as cider of course did), hopped beers were thought to dull the mind and lead you to an early grave). Growing barley to make beer is simply less efficient than growing apples to make cider. Particularly with seventeenth century varieties and technology, you could simply get more pints of cider out of an acre of land than you could pints of beer. John Worlidge, indeed, estimated that an acre of land planted with apple trees would yield more liquor than two or three acres planted with barley. In an age where the ever-present risk of famine was still a recent memory, this was a very important argument. By brewing beer rather than making cider, as Evelyn argued, the nation was wasting its own bread-corn. As well as grain, brewing beer also consumed a great deal of wood as fuel for the boiling process, which was of course not needed for cider making where the sugars are extracted by crushing and pressing rather than boiling. This again was a very pressing concern in the 1650s, with much of England's ancient forests having been used up by the ever growing population. The shift to coal as a domestic fuel had lifted some of the pressure, but England was still forced to turn to Baltic imports of timber to meet the needs of its shipbuilders. This was clearly a great concern for the Royal Society, with Evelyn's *Sylva* (the book to which *Pomona* was appended) focusing on encouraging forestry. In this respect, drinking cider was a win-win situation. Not only did cider not consume fuel in a 'brewing' process, but the orchards themselves yielded wood aplenty as a by-product, which could be put to all kinds of uses from fuel to furniture making.

So, how did these seventeenth century cider pioneers go about finding good cider? Rather than driving round the country in an ever more battered Vauxhall Astra, for them it was a process of scientific enquiry, experimentation, and observation. This had begun as early as the decades before the Civil War when, as other authors have discussed in depth, Herefordshire nobleman Lord Scudamore bred the famous Redstreak apple, and invented the 'Champagne' process which took advantage of advances in glassmaking to produce a sparking bottled cider. Crucially too, finding good cider involved communication: sharing ideas, and disseminating their findings to a wider audience. The seventeenth century had seen the birth of the Royal Mail, making the sending of letters round the country much easier than it had been in the past. Many of the earliest discussions of refining cider emerged out of the circle of correspondents centred on one Samuel Hartlib, with whose encouragement some of the letters were then published as cheap printed tracts (such as Dr. Beal's 1652 work *Herefordshire Orchards: A Pattern For all England*). Later the meetings of the Royal Society came to be the focus of discussions, with many papers on diverse aspects of cider making and orcharding being presented, and some subsequently published in *Pomona*. Clearly wider publication was seen as key to the process. This was not enquiry for enquiry's sake, they wanted their research to make a real difference (what we'd call 'impact' in academia today) and to do this they needed to convince a wider audience of the merits of cider, and to instruct them in the best methods. While not all of their hopes were fulfilled, in this respect they were reasonably successful. *Pomona* went through four editions in Evelyn's lifetime (and many more in the eighteenth and nineteenth centuries) and clearly influenced later works on cider such as John Worlidge's 1676 *Vinetum Britannicum*.

In a lesson which we could do well to learn from today, seventeenth century attempts to find good cider started from the very beginning: with the raw materials. To produce good cider, they needed the best apples, and productive orchards. Their approach to orchards was an interesting one, and resulted in land use which in some respects could be remarkably different from what we think of as 'traditional' orchards today. Scudamore's Redstreak, for example, was a semi-dwarfing tree, and so the recommended planting distance between trees given by Dr. Beal was 15 to 20 foot. This is closer to a modern bush orchard (with a typical spacing of 8-12 foot) than to a 'traditional' standard orchard, where the trees are 30 to 40 foot apart. Such a spacing (Dr. Beal recommended 30-32 foot) was, however, more common for other varieties of apple, and lovers of a tranquil scene will be pleased to hear that both sheep and cattle were commonly grazed amongst the trees. Indeed, one writer even recommended constructing little fort like banks around the trees to protect them from livestock, adding a remark that niggardly farmers would be glad that the incline of the bank meant that they did not actually lose out on grazing surface area!

Although writers such as Ralph Austen valued the tranquillity and natural beauty of orchards, productivity was clearly key. Indeed, the concept of 'improvement' of the land was a widely held ideal, which drove a great deal of agricultural innovation in the seventeenth century. Many cider writers stressed the increased profits which land could yield if turned over to orchards. Ralph Austen for example even suggested that by planting it with fruit trees, the value of land could be increased five, ten, or even twenty fold. They were also keen to slot apple trees into any otherwise un-productive land, such as planting trees in hedgerows, or the headlands which were needed to turn the plough and so usually left uncultivated. In a slightly surprising turn, several writers even recommended a practice which we would today think of as 'intercropping': planting a crop of grain on the orchard floor, and placing the trees fifty to sixty foot apart so that they would not hinder the plough. This again, is a long way from our view of the 'traditional' orchard! Although I can't quite work out the logic (and I did ask a science professor who works on orchards about this) it was widely believed that planting a crop of grain in an orchard improved its productivity, Daniel Colwall for example commenting that 'where land is plow'd and dress'd for Corn, the Trees thrive much better than in Pasture-grounds'. So this was seen as a double benefit, you'd get two crops from the same piece of land, and the apple crop would also be better.

Much thought too was put into choosing the best varieties of apples. The seventeenth century names for apple varieties are both quaint and charming. Some of my favourites are Orange Apple, Golden Ducket, Cat's Head, Violet Apple, and Sodome Apple (also known as Bloudy Pippin for its dark colour). There was clearly a great deal of regional variation, with each of the author's in *Pomona* listing the varieties which were most commonly used in their part of the world. In all by 1676 John Worlidge was able to list at least 77 varieties of apple, many of which were used for making cider, and 11 varieties of perry pear. Of these apples, Scudamore's Redstreak was esteemed above all, producing both high yields and in Evelyn's words the 'richest most vinuous liquor'. Although a long way from the uniformity of Dabinett and Michelin in today's commercial orchards, there was clearly some effort on the part of the members of the Royal Society to advocate the cultivation of what they saw as the best varieties of fruit. As well as extolling their virtues in *Pomona*, some sought to distribute grafts around the country. Dr. Beale, for example, paid out of his own pocket for 20,000 grafts of Redstreak and Genet Moule apples, and Barland pears to be distributed around Somerset, Devon, and Dorset.

Interestingly, the difference between today's West Country style cider (made with bittersweet cider apples) and Eastern style cider (made with low-tannin culinary and dessert fruit) was already well established by the seventeenth century. Sir Paul Neil (who was at the time based in London) for example, wrote in his contribution to *Pomona* that 'Cider made of the best Eating-apples must [be] the best; (that is to say) the pleasantest Cider'. Culinary fruit were certainly grown elsewhere in the country, with Herefordshire's orchards containing both kinds, but table fruit seem to have predominated in the Eastern apple growing counties of Kent and Essex. This was partly a result of difficulties in transportation (with poor-quality roads, the only efficient way to move bulky goods around was by water), and also the lack of technology to preserve perishable fruit. London was crucial as a market for farmers to sell their surplus crops, but for those in the West the only way to get quickly rotting apples to London was by preserving them by turning them into cider. Varieties of apples with high levels of tannins (today's cider apples) were preferable for this, as they acted as a preservative and gave the cider better keeping properties. Counties closer to London, however, could get their fruit to market in a few days, and so were able to grow the dessert varieties which people could eat fresh. As this is what they were growing, it is unsurprising that the Eastern orchardists also used these apples to make cider, and, like Neil, looked for ways to make it the best cider possible (more on which below…).

Moving on to the actual making of cider, perhaps the most striking feature is the multiplicity of methods which were tried, and the lack of agreement amongst the experimental cider makers as to which were the best. When introducing the other author's contributions to *Pomona*, Evelyn even had to go so far as explaining that: 'If some of the following Discourses seem less constant, or (upon occasion) repugnant to one another.... Upon Tryal they may prove grateful to the Public'. Many of their ideas might seem surprising to us today. The diverse range of different ingredients tried out, for example, is a long way from the prescriptive list of those permitted today by HMRC Notice 162, or regarded as 'traditional' by cider purists. Equally we might baulk at some of their techniques; concentrating or diluting juice, and adding sodium metabisulphite to preserve, for example, were commonplace. At a time where innovation and improvement were championed, and there was no strong tradition to fall back on, these ideas were all accepted without question as a potentially valid part of the cidermaker's cannon of techniques, and even embraced as aiding the production of good cider.

Of all of the aspects of cider making, it was the mechanical processes of milling and pressing which received the least attention. Plans for a few innovative presses and devices were presented to the Royal Society, but these do not seem to have had a great impact. Perhaps the most interesting was the 'Ingenio' a mechanical roller mill worked by turning handles, which was patented and marketed by John Worlidge (author of *Vinetum Brittanicum*) in the 1670s. One of the greatest hindrances to the spread of cider making was the high level of technology which was required to make it. Ale, and to a lesser extent hopped beer, could easily be produced on a domestic scale, and indeed in the Middle Ages brewing was traditionally seen as women's work, associated with the well-known figure of the alewife. While ale could be produced in small batches by boiling over a small fire, and used grain which could easily be stored all year, making cider was a much more labour and technologically intensive process. It is possible to by-pass the mill by beating the apples in a trough with wooden poles, but (as anyone who has tried it knows) this is hard work! Even once the apples are crushed, a press is then needed to exert the pressure, further adding to the set up costs to purchase the kit necessary for cider making. Finally, all of the cider had to be made in the autumn as the apples would quickly spoil if kept for more than a few weeks. A large cellar, therefore, was needed to store the whole year's supply, again making cider production a large scale business which simply was not possible on a domestic scale. Although evidence for the Middle Ages is limited, therefore, it seems that before the seventeenth century cider making was likely to have been restricted to those with the capital and space to be able to invest in it. With commercial farming on a reasonable scale still being in its infancy (rather than subsistence peasant production) it seems likely that only large scale landowners such as the monasteries would have been able to make cider. Affordable devices such as Worlidge's Ingenio (priced at around £20, which is about £1,700 in today's money) would have made cider making more accessible. But there is no real evidence that they were adopted on a wide scale. The big horse mills, after all, remained a common sight until well into the twentieth century.

While the crushing and pressing of apples do not seem to have been the subject of great innovation, the seventeenth century cider writers devoted more attention to what happened once the apples had been turned into juice. Very sensibly they had clearly grasped the important point of keeping your cider barrels airtight (probably learnt from the wine makers). More surprising, though, are some of the other measures adopted to enhance the qualities of the juice. Several authors, including Worlidge, Taylor, and Newborough, for example, appear completely unabashed about discussing 'concentrating' the juice by boiling it. Indeed, Worlidge even suggests that this is common practice, remarking that 'in many places they boyl their Cider'. Today concentration is used for ease of storage (as by removing the water, which can easily be added back in later, the concentrated juice takes up less space) but in the seventeenth century it instead seems to have been used to improve the qualities of the juice. With cider often being compared to wine, it is perhaps unsurprising that those seeking a better cider endeavoured to increase its strength. The level of sugars contained in apples mean that cider normally ferments to around 6 or 7 percent ABV, whereas wines are more often 12 to 14 percent. By boiling off half of the water in the juice, therefore, it was possible to create a cider which would ferment to something more akin to a wine strength. Alternatively, with a growing taste for sweeter Spanish wines, it may be that cider makers sought to retain some of the sweetness in this concentrated juice, and make something more like today's ice ciders. Increasing the strength of cider by boiling is referred to by a number of authors, John Newborough for example having 'boil'd away… more than half' and created a drink which after nearly two years he found 'so excessively strong, that five persons would hardly venture upon an ordinary Glass full of it'. Indeed, there do seem to have been widespread doubts about the merits of boiling cider, with John Worlidge remarking that 'this way is not to be commended' because the juice developed a 'high colour' and an ill flavour.

Cider Brandy (fine though it is) is a completely different topic, so I won't discuss its heritage here. While it was clearly made in seventeenth century England, the widespread consumption of distilled drinks was still in its infancy at this stage, and was not to really take off in England until the eighteenth century 'Gin Craze'. I do, though, have to mention one entrepreneur, Richard Haines, who in 1684 patented a new way of making a new wine strength cider based drink, a drink which he called Cyder Royal. This was made by double distilling a hogshead of cider, and then mixing this back in to another hogshead of cider to create something which is more like a fortified wine, or today's cider brandy aperitifs. Sadly, however, it never really caught on.

While the use of concentrated juice is controversial today, adding in water is equally often decried, with many favouring a 100 percent juice approach. Such dilution of cider, however, has an equally long history, clearly being widely practiced in the seventeenth century. Evelyn, for example, remarked that 'some Cider mixeth kindly with water in the cider-mill, and will hold out a good small wine'. The idea is discussed in greatest depth, however, by Worlidge who devoted a whole section of *Vinetum Britannicum* to the making of 'Water-Cider', also called 'Ciderkin'. This was done by taking pomace which had already been pressed once and rehydrating it with boiled water. After about 48 hours this could then be re-pressed, yielding a lower strength cider which would 'supply the place of Small-Beer in a Family'. Ciderkin was probably around 2-3 percent ABV, and hence did not have particularly good keeping qualities, something which Worlidge suggested remedying by boiling it up with hops which would act as a preservative. This, perhaps, is the root of the reason why we cannot come to clear definitions of what constitutes 'real' cider today. Should it be a full juice wine like drink, or should it be a weaker 'long' drink like beer which can be consumed by the pint. The historian's answer is simply that it is and was both of these. Depending on the way in which it is prepared, apples can yield both a strong full juice drink to take the place of wine on the master's table, and a weaker watered down drink to refresh the farm labourers or give to the children. This is a practice which has at least a 400 year history, and if we accept this multiplicity of definitions (that both artisan and industrial ciders are 'traditional') it may be easier to work out exactly what we mean by 'cider' today.

While I'm in the process of destroying the purists notions of what constitutes 'traditional' practice in cider making, I may as well point out that the use of the dreaded 'sulphites' in cider (Camden Tablets to any home brewers) also dates back to the seventeenth century! Worlidge, for example, remarked that 'if before cider be tunned up into it, the vessel be fumed with Sulphur, it much conduceth to the preservation of this or any other kind of liquor'. A similar process was also described by Dr. Beale: 'As sulphur hath some use in wines, so some do lay Brimstone on a rage, and when the Vessel is full of Smoak, the liquor speedily poured in ferments the better.' While, like many today, he clearly had doubts about this practice, he concluded that: 'I cannot condemn this, for Sulphur is more kind to the lungs than Cider, and the impurity will be discharged in the ferment.'

At least, I'm sure a sizeable proportion of my readers are hoping, he surely can't say that these noxious fruit 'ciders' are traditional! Sorry, they are too I'm afraid! Although (cue sight of relief!) not all approved of the practice, many of the seventeenth century cider authors refer to adding various fruits and spices to cider, clearly suggesting that it was a widespread practice. Dr. Beal, for example, while commenting that 'generally the gentry of Herefordshire do abhor mixtures', variously suggests the addition of ginger, mustard, rosemary, and bays to cider to correct various faults. While he disliked the taste of juniper berries, to add additional flavours into cider Beal also discussed mixing in raspberries, cherries, plums, and clove-July flowers. Sylas Taylor displayed similarly mixed opinions, stating that: 'I am against the boyling of cider, or the hanging of a bag of spices in it, or the use of ginger in drinking it', but also arguing that 'mingled with the syrup of Raspberries it makes an excellent woman's wine'. The most detailed discussion comes from John Worlidge who, while he argued that 'there is not any liquor that hath less need of Mixtures than Cider, being of it self so excellent, that any addition whatsoever maketh it less pleasant', also advocated cider as 'the most proper vehicle' to transfer the medicinal virtues of a range of fruits and spices into the body. While those proposing Motion 19 at CAMRA's 2015 AGM were, therefore, completely right in citing texts such as *Vinetum Britannicum* to argue that fruit, spiced, and hopped ciders have a long history, they do need to be a little careful in understanding how this practice was used. Clearly most use of spices in particular was to correct faults or for medicinal reasons, and was decried by many. While this is 'traditional' therefore, I'm not really sure if it fits with the quest for high quality premium products rather than 'bland processed beers' which CAMRA apply to Real Ale.

While some of the practices described above perhaps do not sit easily with our modern notions of 'good cider', some of the other practices developed in the seventeenth century certainly do! Let's finish, then, by discussing premium bottled products. I've already referred to Lord Scudamore's experiments in developing the 'Champagne' process in the 1630s. By the 1650s and 60s, this seems to have become common practice, and is referred to by many of the cider makers, who recommend adding a handful of raisons or 'as much as a walnut' of sugar so that it continues to ferment in bottle. The process is perhaps best described by Sir Paul Neil who wrote that: 'When it is bottled it must not be perfectly fine, for if it be so, it will not fret in the bottle, which gives it a fine quickness, and will make it mantle and sparkle in the glass when you pour it out'.

One of my favourite recent discoveries whilst perusing the seventeenth century cider literature is that they were also experimenting with the process which we today call keeving, or French style cider making. That is causing a cap to form on top of the cider which strips out some of the nutrients, then syphoning it off from underneath to give a clear, low nutrient juice which will ferment slowly enough to retain some residual sweetness and, when bottled, a pleasant sparkle. Several of the contributors to *Pomona* refer to removing the 'flying lee' which would form on top of the cider (a term which I think is much more romantic than the French 'chapeaux brun' (or 'brown hat')), and the process was described in greater depth in a pair of papers by Sir Paul Neil. These discussions are fascinating, and in an odd way also rather charming, as, although the explanations they give for why it was happening are a long way from our modern day understanding of the keeving process, by simple observation and experimentation they had clearly discovered a highly effective way of making good cider!

When you yourself, then, go out seeking good ciders, remember that you are continuing a long-standing and noble tradition. One too, which was seen as worthy of the attention of some of the finest minds of their time. Our attitudes to cider, the ways we make it, and even the qualities of the drink itself have doubtlessly changed much over the years. Indeed, many aspects of cider making which we view as 'authentic' and 'traditional' would have seemed like outlandish innovations to the cider makers of four hundred years ago. Equally, several 'innovations' which we today revile would have been seen as perfectly acceptable in cider's 'Golden Age'. What we certainly have in common, though, is the quest for perfection, and a passion for this most pleasant of drinks. So, next time you sit down with a pint of your favourite tipple, pause for a moment and raise a toast to those first pioneers who started out on the quest to find good cider, and did so much to shape the development of a drink which so many enjoy today.

Finding Good Cider

Index

Producers – (many omissions and errors excepted!)

Cider Pubs and Venues

Finding Good Cider